Praise for *The Three Sisters of the Tao*

*"**The Three Sisters of the Tao** is a pleasure tonic and a life-giving elixir designed to help all of us remember how life is supposed to be felt and lived. I loved it."*

— **Christiane Northrup, M.D.,** the author of
The Secret Pleasures of Menopause and
Women's Bodies, Women's Wisdom

"Terah Kathryn Collins trusts the poetry of everyday life to reveal the boundless potential for a meaningful and pleasurable existence. She has achieved a point of view where she's open to the magic of every moment, and her book invites you to join her."

— **Thomas Moore,** the author of *Care of the Soul* and *Writing in the Sand*

The
Three Sisters
of the Tao

ALSO BY TERAH KATHRYN COLLINS

Books

HOME DESIGN WITH FENG SHUI A–Z

THE WESTERN GUIDE TO FENG SHUI

THE WESTERN GUIDE TO FENG SHUI FOR PROSPERITY

THE WESTERN GUIDE TO FENG SHUI FOR ROMANCE
(book-with-CD)

THE WESTERN GUIDE TO FENG SHUI, Room by Room

Audio Program

INTRODUCTION TO FENG SHUI

All of the above are available at your local bookstore,
or may be ordered by visiting:

Hay House USA: **www.hayhouse.com®**
Hay House Australia: **www.hayhouse.com.au**
Hay House UK: **www.hayhouse.co.uk**
Hay House South Africa: **www.hayhouse.co.za**
Hay House India: **www.hayhouse.co.in**

The Three Sisters of the Tao

of the

Essential Conversations with
Chinese Medicine, I Ching, and Feng Shui

TERAH KATHRYN COLLINS

HAY HOUSE, INC.
Carlsbad, California • New York City
London • Sydney • Johannesburg
Vancouver • Hong Kong • New Delhi

Published and distributed in the United States by: Hay House, Inc.: www.hay house.com • *Published and distributed in Australia by:* Hay House Australia Pty. Ltd.: www.hayhouse.com.au • *Published and distributed in the United Kingdom by:* Hay House UK, Ltd.: www.hayhouse.co.uk • *Published and distributed in the Republic of South Africa by:* Hay House SA (Pty), Ltd.: www .hayhouse.co.za • *Distributed in Canada by:* Raincoast: www.raincoast.com • *Published in India by:* Hay House Publishers India: www.hayhouse.co.in

Editorial supervision: Jill Kramer • *Project editor:* Jessica Kelley
Design: Jami Goddess • *Interior illustrations:* Terah Kathryn Collins

The author of this book does not dispense medical advice or prescribe the use of any technique as a form of treatment for physical, emotional, or medical problems without the advice of a physician, either directly or indirectly. The intent of the author is only to offer information of a general nature to help you in your quest for emotional and spiritual well-being. In the event you use any of the information in this book for yourself, which is your constitutional right, the author and the publisher assume no responsibility for your actions.

Library of Congress Cataloging-in-Publication Data

Collins, Terah Kathryn.
  The three sisters of the Tao : essential conversations with Chinese medicine, I Ching, and feng shui / Terah Kathryn Collins.
       p. cm.
  ISBN 978-1-4019-1684-8 (tradepaper : alk. paper) 1. Taoism--Philosophy. 2. Yi jing. 3. Feng shui. 4. Medicine, Chinese. I. Title.
  BF175.4.R44C653 2010
  181'.114--dc22   2009044181

ISBN: 978-1-4019-1684-8

13 12 11 10   4 3 2 1
1st edition, June 2010

Printed in the United States of America

To Carolyn Smith Beatson,
who knew the Way

Contents

PART I: Essential Conversations with the Three Sisters of the Tao

PART II: 22 Essential Pearls from the Three Sisters of the Tao

Author's Note

The essence of what began in my journals and developed into meditative dialogues with the Three Sisters of the Tao is contained in this book. It's an experiential exploration of the philosophical foundation out of which Chinese Medicine, I Ching, and Feng Shui were born: one woman's deep "see" dive into the *essential underpinnings* beneath each Sister's worldly manifestations over the past several thousand years.

Interpretations of certain details about the Sisters—including family placement, personality traits, physical attributes, and special interests—are my subjective interpretation of their individuality.

Part I includes my conversations with the Sisters and their Seeds of Transformation, essential thoughts and phrases from each dialogue. While some of the Seeds are quite similar, each carries its own particular resonant meaning. Please refer to Essential Pearls #7, #14, and #21 for specific suggestions on how to apply the Seeds in your life.

The 22 Essential Pearls in Part II offer a collection of meditations and introspective activities meant to deepen your personal experience of this material.

I offer this book to you as an open invitation to plumb the luminous depths of your heart, the home of your true self, and beyond. May you discover many inner and outer treasures along the Way. . . .

Preface

Your Heart Is Where Your Home Is

When it comes to an experiential adventure, the Three Sisters of the Tao are forces to be reckoned with. They've taken to heart my desire to live in enduring harmony and led me down the Class-5 rapids of transformation. As expert guides, they're calm, highly skilled way-showers who continue to teach me how to navigate through the uncertainties of life using the inner compass of the heart.

Translated as "the Way," the Tao chronicles the path of harmony. As Sisters, Chinese Medicine, I Ching, and Feng Shui are born from the Tao, their legacies tracing back as far as the historical eye can see. There's a timeless quality about their message that's easy to recognize. *We can feel it.* The Tao, the Way, is permeated with love.

I feel that each Sister offers her own perspective. Chinese Medicine places tranquility at the very core of the Way. She's poetic in her observations, viewing the body as a temple of miracles where the tranquil heart is the bedchamber of

Heaven and Earth and the home of the true self. She counsels us to embrace a balanced lifestyle where work, play, and rest form a trinity from which our full potential can blossom. Many inner gateways open in her healing presence, invitations to embody myriad facets of our selves as imaginative, sensual, luminous human beings.

I Ching views kindness as the heart of the matter. She's fierce in her direction, lest we sink in the dark waters of heartlessness. She tutors us in weaving kindness into every thought, word, and action, a practice that circles around to sow all manner of blessings into our lives. She's also a revealer, unveiling the nonphysical world of loving help devoted to our ever-unfolding transformations.

Feng Shui gathers the wisdom of her Sisters and brings it home. She encourages us to personally craft environmental sanctuaries that can hold our true selves in place. A great enthusiast of comfort, safety, and beauty, she's always looking for ways to give kindness and imagination shelter. Through her influence, our inner and outer worlds become harmonious reflections of each other, resonant chords in a living symphony of sacred space within the greater matrix of community.

Having been a Feng Shui author and teacher since 1995, I know how to work with the five elements of wood, fire, earth, metal, and water found in Chinese Medicine; and the I Ching's eight basic trigrams related to prosperity, recognition, love, creativity, synchronicity, purpose, wisdom, and vitality. Although they both provide many indispensable tools in the practice of Feng Shui, it didn't occur to me to delve more deeply into their wisdom or origin. I was preoccupied, the insistent prodding of multiple deadlines my constant companions.

Opportunities to write, lecture, develop curricula, and teach formed a growing circle around my life, looked in my windows, knocked on my door, and kept me awake at night. I was overwhelmed by the work I loved; I was a well going dry in a heat wave of opportunity. Surrounded by people cheering me on, I pushed harder, dove deeper, became emptier and emptier . . . until three revealing messages conspired to restore my balance.

The first arrived one evening while having dinner with a friend. "I wake up in the morning and wait for something to pull me," she said. "I'm choosing not to respond to an outer push anymore, only to the inner pull." She moved as though she were being shoved from behind when she said "push," and touched her heart as her chest lifted when she said "pull."

As I listened, a tidal wave of recognition washed over me. My entire life was about being pushed! God forbid I wait for some inner pull when I could just keep pressing forward. In that moment, I was overcome by the heartlessness of so much pushing. An image of an incarcerated woman flashed before my eyes, along with an absolute knowing: I was living in a prison of my own making.

I began to assess my life through the lens of push or pull. Everywhere I looked, I saw another demanding push defining the landscape of my life. An inner mutiny was brewing. The prison guard was having a hard time containing the prisoner, who was waking up and wanting out.

Soon after, the second message arrived while I was standing in the bathroom with my husband, Brian. I was struck by the exaggerated difference between our reflections in the mirror. My hair was painfully short, while his flowed to his shoulders. The long-haired man appeared happy, while the hollow-eyed woman with the cropped hair looked wasted. There she was—the prisoner I'd glimpsed before—staring back at me in the mirror.

The third message was delivered a few days later when a high fever forced me into bed. Delirious, I floated through a stream of childhood memories. Each seemed quite ordinary, but as I journeyed along, I became increasingly aware of a foreboding feeling permeating each scene. Family meals, school days, and times with friends were all infused with the same disturbing vibration. Everything looked fine on the surface, but something was very wrong. What was it? The answer punched me hard in the chest. *Everybody's heart was broken.*

I'd never looked at my life from this perspective before, but there it was—my middle-class, suburban upbringing in the 1950s and '60s was essentially a study of the brokenhearted. My parents' hearts were lost long before I was born.

They raised their two daughters in an atmosphere that swung between tense silences and caustic exchanges—the same way they'd grown up. Their chronic misery and unkindness toward each other was considered completely normal, a condition that seemed to pervade every household in our neighborhood.

Heartless words and the thoughts that fueled them permeated our home and community, an acidic counterpoint to the faux sweetness we were expected to display to others. Any thin veneer of pleasantness easily peeled away to reveal the dark underbelly of unkindness in my teachers, neighbors, family members, and friends. We were all soaked in it, colored by it. By the time I was a teenager, my heart sufficiently matched those around me. Plied with drugs and alcohol, I learned to stay numb and trust no one.

My febrile exploration continued into adulthood, where the same disheartening behaviors prevailed in the New Age people I spent time with. Rhetorical enlightenment provided no real heart repair. Without our inner compasses intact, we were all lost. Casting about for some sense of direction and release from the stranglehold of destructive behaviors, I traveled to faraway places and lived in several communes. I learned a dozen ways to meditate and attended innumerable workshops, looking for a way to be something—anything—other than perpetually numb.

The first signs of regaining some sensation emerged when I learned to literally feel through my hands as a massage and polarity therapist. My practice spanned a dozen years as I married, divorced, and married again. I experienced life as hard work, my outer challenges reflecting my inner process. Chipping my way out of steely numbness was slow and laborious, light penetrating through one tiny opening at a time.

With my move to California in 1990 came more changes, including another divorce and a career transformation. As my second marriage ended, a new beginning came my way. I was introduced to Feng Shui and felt, for the first time, a real passion coursing through my veins. I leapt into it with newfound enthusiasm, the holistic principles of working with the human body making my studies of the environmental body a series of thrilling *Ahas*. Feng Shui was written in my bones! I was on fire, and my life ignited around me.

I met Louise Hay, and our friendship blossomed. After hearing enough Feng Shui stories from me, she suggested I author a book about my experiences. Published in early 1996, *The Western Guide to Feng Shui* surprised everyone by quickly becoming a bestseller, jetting me into the fast lane.

Now, after more than a decade of manic productivity, I was in bed, certain I was reviewing my life before dying. But I *wasn't* dying. My fever was peaking, and as it did, a peculiar image slowly floated toward me. The closer it got, the more it looked like a burnt chicken gizzard. When I realized what it really was, I burst into tears. It was my heart.

My journey down memory lane, with its poignant focus on the general condition of the people's hearts in my world, had illuminated the sad state of my own. I lay in bed in complete shock as the grand finale of my delirium rolled by—a vast view of generations of children, their loving natures crushed like fragile filigree beneath the heavy boots of the brokenhearted. . . .

Finally, I slept and had a vivid dream. I was a feral cat crouched in the bushes outside a house. It was night, and golden light streamed from every window. A curious sign, reading YOUR HEART IS WHERE YOUR HOME IS, hung over the front door. A beautiful woman stepped out with a bowl of warm milk. Behind her, two more women watched from a candlelit room.

"Here, sweetheart, this is for you," she called softly as she looked in my direction and set down the bowl. I waited until she went inside, then leaped for the milk. Gulping my fill, I heard the woman say, "She's so ready to come home."

Indeed, I was ready, and as I awoke from this dream, I realized that I had absolutely no idea how to get there. Seeing the condition of my heart was like an electroshock treatment, impossible to forget. I was going to have to slow down and ask for help—except slowing down was a punishable sin to me, and asking for help was a sure sign of weakness. I felt like a prodigal daughter—starved, bedraggled, and a long way from home.

I recalled a neighbor saying that she lingered in bed every morning with a cup of tea. This simple act, one I'd previously judged as a complete waste of time, now struck me as the perfect way to begin. I fetched some tea and crawled back into my warm bed. I thought about the push and pull, the font of revealing images and memories, the three women, and the famished cat. Then something across the room caught my attention. There, practically waving from the bookshelf, was the I Ching, my first pull toward home.

The I Ching, translated as "The Book of Transformations," provides guidance on restoring and sustaining harmony with Nature and the Cosmos. A treatise on the Way, it quickly became my morning bedfellow. One by one, I worked with the I Ching's 64 hexagrams (lessons), for a week or more, identifying my misunderstandings about the Way and incrementally correcting them.

It was intense work, beginning each morning in bed, continuing through the rest of the day, and shaping my dreams. It was a kick-ass, tough-love recovery program, combined with enough inspiration to set me reeling. I was compelled to follow the path it laid before me. Little by little, the grueling self-inquiry laced with revelation was rehabilitating my heart, and my life was changing to reflect it. I stuck with the work, encouraged by the flicker of loving-kindness that began to lighten the atmosphere within and around me.

Soon, Chinese Medicine joined our morning rendezvous, instructing me on the alchemy of the body. Her soothing, poetic portrayals of the corporeal terrain helped me relax and go with the flow of my healing process. We sometimes stayed in bed for hours, my journals filling up with our daily sojourns.

Feng Shui, who had lived with me for well over a decade, was a comforting presence in our horizontal study halls. I grew to love our time together. There was no rushing or pushing toward a goal with these three. I surrendered to the unhurried pace of their guidance and care.

One day it clicked: Chinese Medicine, I Ching, and Feng Shui were the three women in my dream—and they're Sisters of the Tao. Their close family resemblance had become evident in our morning sessions, their message essentially the same: My heart is where my home is. *Love is the Way.*

My transformation from the feral way to the Cosmic Way continues. Incrementally, my leaden self turns to gold. Simplicity, pleasure, and kindness are my spiritual practices on a path of *being* rather than *doing*.

No longer numb, I can now feel the distinction between push and pull, and kindly let pushy influences rush by. The wings of my imagination have returned, lifting me into a whole new realm of creative potency. Morning meditation and sunset journaling bracket my days as I learn to think with my heart, feel with my mind, and walk with the cadence of kindness.

More and more, friendly playfulness replaces feral shyness. Instead of avoiding interactions with others, I'm drawn to them, sharing sweet moments with strangers and friends alike. Everyday life as improvisational theater has my full attention, each moment providing another unique opportunity to observe and participate in the play. The ordinary has become extraordinary. I watch parents walk their babies, pelicans fly overhead, kids and dogs frolic, and sunsets color the sky; and I'm swept into the sheer beauty of it all. Tears flow easily, healing waters washing more gristle and ashes from my heart.

In the world of the Three Sisters of the Tao, all hearts are cherished. As the abode of your true self, your inner compass, and your personal link with Nature and the Cosmos, your heart is the center of your humanity. With a loving-kindness you may not yet know . . .

> *The Three Sisters of the Tao*
> *Reach out to touch you*
> *This time to wake you*
> *Gently so you remember*
> *Your heart is where your home is . . .*

Introduction

THREE SISTERS OF THE TAO PARABLE

Once upon a time, long, long ago, Mother Earth looked up into the sparkling eyes and dazzling smile of Father Heaven and fell deeply in love. Father Heaven gazed down upon Mother Earth's sensuous curves and alluring beauty; and he, too, fell in love. They wrapped their arms around each other and became the Tao, the Way; the marriage of Heaven and Earth; the eternal loving union of the visible and invisible worlds.

Soon, their firstborn arrived. Her parents recognized her luminous tranquility as the sign of a healer, and named her *Chinese Medicine*. Being her mother's daughter, she embodied the soothing serenity that could restore the natural balance of every person, animal, plant, and mineral on Earth. Being her father's daughter, she inspired every heart to fully open and flower, making all healing possible. And from the moment Chinese Medicine was born, she could return even the most burdened souls to their true lightness of being.

Mother Earth and Father Heaven's second child was born with light blazing from her amber eyes, the sign of a teacher. They named her *I Ching,* meaning "to transform." Being her mother's daughter, she embodied the graceful ability to reveal the unique gifts in every person, animal, plant, and mineral on Earth. Being her father's daughter, she could illuminate every heart, making fluency in loving-kindness possible. And from the moment I Ching was born, she could teach even the clumsiest of souls the flowing dance of their true selves.

When the third child entered the world, her parents recognized her keen interest in her surroundings as the sign of an environmental healer. They named her *Feng Shui,* meaning "wind and water." Being her mother's daughter, she embodied the magical practicality that could breathe new life into the habitats of every person, animal, plant, and mineral on Earth. Being her father's daughter, she lightened every heart, expanding the continuum of love in all directions. And from the moment Feng Shui was born, she could guide even the most lost of souls home.

Like their parents, the Three Sisters were inseparable and loved to share their gifts with each other. Chinese Medicine inspired her family with the healing songs and poems from the hearts of tiny birds, mighty trees, and people of every race. I Ching choreographed enchanting dances to further bring the healing songs and poems to life, and Feng Shui created fanciful sets for their magical improvisations.

One day, Mother Earth and Father Heaven called their three daughters to them and gave them each a garment. "These are the robes you'll wear when you cross from the

East to the West," said Mother Earth. "Your Father and I have woven them equally from the threads of Earth and Heaven to guide and illuminate your Way."

Father Heaven embraced his daughters and said, "Your Mother and I have also sewn the seeds of transformation into the hems of your robes. As you move through the world, they'll be planted along the Way."

They wrapped Chinese Medicine in a jade green robe, intricately embellished with long silver threads and imbued with the luminous essence of tranquility. I Ching was gently draped in an ivory silk robe covered with hearts of spun gold and adorned with the bright flames of clarity. And they enfolded Feng Shui in a robe colorfully embroidered with waterfalls, forests, and temples and infused with the sweet elixir of joy.

The Sisters made their way to the West, where they now offer their gifts to you. They recognize you as a love child of Mother Earth and Father Heaven, connected heart to heart with all other beings. They embrace you as their brother or sister and honor the unique part you play in the circle of life. And in the spirit of the Tao, the Three Sisters celebrate the Way that is *your* way and the gifts *you* bring into the world.

And so it is and always shall be.

PART I

Essential Conversations
with the
Three Sisters
of the *Tao*

Eternal Circle of Life
(Courtesy Terah Kathryn Collins)

CHAPTER ONE

Love lives here
In the tranquil heart

Sanctuary of Heaven and Earth
Shelters the true self

Flights of fancy; sweet belonging
Flow on serenity's stream

Chinese Medicine sits in tranquil repose in the middle of a large circle. She appears to be lit from within, her jade robe and long ebony hair cascading around her. Her eyes drift open, and I look into a world of sylvan green serenity.

She invites me into the circle, her voice like a temple bell. As I sit across from her, I slip out of my own shadow and into the light.

She begins to speak softly: "Your heart is your true home, and your desire to return to it serves you well. Together with my Sisters, I am here to guide your Way."

She gently takes my hands. "The Way of your true self is this: you are a temple of miracles, a living altar of soul and cells. As a love child of Heaven and Earth, you are angel and animal entwined, a creative genius illuminating cellular structure.

"When you look through the eyes of your true self, you see your flesh and spirit as equals, merging as creature and creator. Your body is Heaven's feet and your spirit, Earth's wings. Through you, they express and embody the Way."

I feel the poetry of her words resonate through my body. I lean toward her, longing for more.

"Your heart, the sanctuary of Heaven and Earth, is the home of your true self. As you rekindle your heart, the wonder and majesty of life returns. Your spirit arises from a dark cloud of amnesia, and you soar once again into the boundless expanses of your imagination. Your body awakens from the anesthesia of the past, transforming numbness into streams of pleasure. The voices of your senses become crystal clear, guiding you to further joy. Reunited once again with the full circle of life, your heart becomes the enchanted abode where Heaven and Earth's beloved offspring—you—can thrive."

Her words arouse the memory of a recent early-morning dream. I'm a small child looking at a circle of people who

4

stand close together holding hands. I feel painfully shy, and a keen sense of loneliness fills me until I notice a woman and a man standing on either side of me. They gently smile and hold out their hands. For a moment, I'm paralyzed, the sharp desire to reach out colliding with my shyness. Then I reach up and take their hands. We approach the circle, and it opens to include us. I feel completely surrounded by love, the sense of belonging intensifying until it wakes me up.

"This is how it happens," Chinese Medicine says, her calm face lit with a smile. "It begins with the remembrance of how love really feels. Incrementally, each memory and moment helps you reclaim your true nature; and as you do, your heart is restored."

I feel a stiff binding around my heart loosen, like a tight corset falling away. I breathe deeply into the physical relief, savoring the new sense of freedom in my body.

"Yes, let your heart breathe—it becomes more spacious with every breath you take." Chinese Medicine closes her eyes and rests her hands in her lap, inviting me to do the same. "The radiant essences of Heaven and Earth are always streaming around you, and now you are learning how to open your inner gateways and invite them to flow into you. As you breathe, feel them flow into your body from above and below, merge in your heart, and expand out through every cell of your body and beyond. . . ."

As she speaks, I feel ribbons of light travel up through my pelvis and down through my head, filling my heart with warm bursts of energy. This continues with every breath I take, bathing me in washes of pleasure. I feel completely relaxed and euphoric at the same time. Astonished, I open my eyes and find her smiling.

"When your heart is open, you become the creative conduit of Heaven and Earth. Through you, they are prolific! They cause inspiration and sensuality to merge within you, calling forth your true self. You begin to see the rolling landscapes of music, hear the poetry of paintings, savor the taste of colors, and revel in the fragrant bouquets of words. You become the explorer of your own endless wilderness. The fluid intermingling of Heaven and Earth within you enhances the potency of your work, the sensations in your body, and the depth of your inner sojourns."

She lets silence embrace us for a moment, then says, "Harmony is made from the threads of pleasure you weave into your everyday experiences. The more these strands intricately embellish the matrix of your daily life, the better. Your work, play, and rest are a trinity of influences that all contribute to the tapestry of your life. By honoring them as equals, you balance the synergy of your body and spirit and restore the natural grace of *being* a human being."

She pauses again, letting her words find a place to rest within me, then continues. "Most children know instinctively how to enjoy everything they do. When they work, they focus all their attention on accomplishing a task, such as building a sand castle or solving a puzzle. You can see how intently engaged they are in their work. They also know how to be wildly creative and imaginative, having parties with invisible friends, inventing games, and becoming heroes and animals in every kind of playful fantasy. And when they are ready for rest, they can fall sound asleep anywhere."

Silence envelops us once more. When she speaks, I can feel her lyrical voice streaming through my body as much as I hear her words. "Work often has an active, laserlike quality that calls you to be productive and accomplish specific tasks that require a focused output of energy. This can be full of the pleasures of manifestation and the fulfillment of completion. Because you are the steward of your own well-being, it is your quest to seek out and magnify the threads of joy in your work."

She leans toward me and looks deeply into my eyes. "You are meant to be life enjoying itself—life, loving life. Be always generous with the gift of time. Hurrying is like a strong wind rattling the windows and doors of your heart. When such a gale howls continually, your harmony is swept away. You leave the halcyon climate of the Way and enter the storm whenever you squeeze time and leave it breathless."

How unkind of me! I want to hold time in my arms and apologize for how often I've hurried it along.

"You resuscitate time when you let every day be an invitation rather than a forced march," Chinese Medicine explains. "You are a human being, not a human doing. Even during your work, let hurrying become a thing of the past and leave time to meander between your commitments. Enchantment awaits you there."

She bathes me in her serene gaze for several moments, watching the space for enchantment to open up within me, then offers: "While work is focused on productivity, play naturally follows the amorphous slipstream of pleasure. Here, you engage in the activities that bring you joy, feast on gatherings with favorite friends and family members, cavort with the ever-flowing font of your creativity, and relish the pastimes that make your heart sing.

"Your rest, sleep, and introspection sustain your tranquility. Here, you open up the space to commune with your inner helpers, whose whispers can only be heard in silence. Your daydreams and night dreams are some of their gifts to you, numinous signs guiding you along the Way. Rest gives you time to lie in your own arms and feel who you are. When you are in repose, your connection with Heaven and Earth is restored and deepened so that your heart remains tranquil and open to the pleasures of your work and play."

I wonder about the inner helpers she mentioned, and she says, "I Ching will instruct you on your inner world and much more, while Feng Shui will help you integrate your studies into the outer world. Your first step is to bring the balance of rest, play, and work into your everyday life, because everything you are learning is built upon this foundation. As you discovered with your work, an imbalanced lifestyle can extinguish delight and disturb your equilibrium."

Yes, it can. I think of my many hapless years dedicated solely to labor. Between my family's compulsive work ethic and the cultural leaning toward productivity, I learned to make it the most important part of my life, the supreme "Doing." Pleasure had nothing to do with it, and in fact, was suspect. It didn't belong there. Playtime had to be earned and was closely monitored for excess. Like many people, I thought this was the "right" way to live, nose to the grindstone every waking moment.

"Your lifestyle was hierarchical rather than humane. When work reigns, you sacrifice your tranquility and sensuality, thinking it makes you more productive . . . until you discover such an arrangement has little duration. Only balance endures." Her face is lit with compassion. "The mistakes you have made in the past become the wisdom that carries you into the future. Not one day has been wasted. Everything you have learned serves you well.

"Treasure the blessings inherent in every moment," she says, her soothing voice calling me deep inside myself. "Celebrate the ever-unfolding love affair between your spirit and flesh. Let your imagination soar, gather what was once unimaginable, and return ecstatic. Invite your creative genius to shape every moment. Be gracious to your body and offer her what she asks for—a walk in the sunshine, a rest in the middle of the day, a favorite flavor. Infuse being into doing. It is more than taking the time to smell the roses; it is giving yourself the space to sink fully into the mystery of the roses, and all of life. Make this your daily practice. Your kind attendance to your inner and outer worlds—your entire being—restores your heart and calls forth the full expression of who you are."

As I listen to her, dark chunks of misery break free and float away while inner gateways open. I can feel how shut down I've been. As a small child, I was wide open to life, finely tuned and constantly engaged. From arranging food on a plate to building fairy castles in the woods, I was an ever-flowing, pleasure-seeking font of creativity. Even when I had to endure sensory distress, I could imagine myself in more pleasant circumstances. My flights of imagination were my saving grace. What happened?

A vivid memory emerges: I'm sitting at a cramped wooden desk under the glare and buzz of fluorescent lights, listening to a teacher's dull monologue. The smell of rancid shepherd's pie hangs in the dank air. I'm eight years old; and for the last three years of my life, I've had variations of this repugnant experience hundreds of times. I'm in deep sensory distress. My eyes, ears, nose, and skin are all on red alert, signaling me for relief. I look out at patches of sky through the high windows and imagine being in the woods near my house. I see myself walking along the stream and climbing my favorite tree. The fresh air, quiet gurgle of water, and scent of warm leaves begin to work their magic. I breathe it all in with great relief, just as a shout catapults me back into the room.

I realize that the teacher and the other students are all staring at me. The teacher scowls and shouts again, "Yes, you—you are *not* allowed to daydream in this class!"

I hang my head, mortified. Everyone is snickering, amused by my embarrassment. I cringe in my chair and feel an overwhelming sense of loss, as though something precious within me is dying.

That day, I lost the ability to temper the ongoing barrage of offensive experiences in my life. Daydreaming had been a lifeline for my survival, and when my imaginary rope broke, I went numb. And now the ramifications become clear. My heavenly imagination and my earthly instinct to seek pleasure are expressions of my true self. When I lost them, I lost the key to my heart.

Chinese Medicine gently touches my hands, bringing my attention back into the circle. "Like many children, the wings of your imagination were clipped while your body struggled to survive. Unable to soar or land, anxiety replaced tranquility, your true self dwindled, and your heart became dark and still."

I picture an abandoned house haunted with sad memories. Her comforting touch holds me steady.

"Kiss the past and let it go. You are breathing new life into your heart, and it is warming and brightening. You have opened the door and strewn petals across the threshold. You have lit candles in all the windows. You are restoring your inner abode to its original splendor, and it is beginning to take shape. Come, let us take a look . . ."

We close our eyes. She gently lets go of my hands and says, "Your heart is your inner sanctuary. It dwells within the ever-evolving paradise you imagine into being, and it is infused with everything you cherish. . . ."

I listen to the murmur of her voice and find I'm walking down a dappled path toward a gateway, ornately carved with a magnificent pair of wings. I am struck by how beautiful they are and am filled with longing. If I could have wings, I could have anything.

"You can," I hear Chinese Medicine whisper. "Reclaim the wings of your imagination and ride the currents of feeling into your inner world. The sanctuary of your heart is not so much *thought* as *felt* into being. Fill it with love, love, and more love."

I swing the gate open and step through, opening myself to the treasure chest of things I love. Iridescence—the ethereal beauty that glimmers in hummingbird feathers and abalone shells—sparkles all around me. I feel giddy, the complete freedom to create my inner sanctuary flooding me with possibilities. It can be however I wish!

A spectacular pavilion, intricately carved with flora and fauna, appears—a work of art set in panoramic gardens. Silk couches and pillows in iridescent jewel tones appoint the pavilion's open-air interior. Ocean views abound; turquoise waters and lacy white waves encircle an archipelago of islands. Garden paths wend their way down to the beach, while a waterfall pours its music into a nearby pool. . . .

"As you breathe life into your inner world, it takes on a vitality of its own," Chinese Medicine whispers. "It breathes life back into you. Tend to it and revel in all the details— the architecture, atmosphere, colors, fragrances, sounds, and textures. Imagine them more and more into being. Be ever enchanted as you drink in the layers of astonishing beauty that your choices create. They are solely and eternally yours." Her voice blends with the murmur of water, and I feel my inner and outer worlds become one complete circle.

"The circle is a beautiful metaphor for life. . . ."

I open my eyes and watch Chinese Medicine motion slowly around the circle where we sit.

"In your dream, you held hands with Heaven and Earth and stepped into your Circle of Belonging. For a moment, you fully embodied your true self. Now you are making your dream come true."

As she speaks, I recall the circle of people with the woman and man by my side. The loving embrace of that gathering touches me again, bringing tears to my eyes.

"You can expand moments like those in your dream until they become your entire experience. Whenever you are agitated or distressed, remember your dream and gently enfold yourself in the *feeling* of the circle. Take this sensation of deep and abiding belonging into your inner sanctuary and let it ignite the heart of your imagination. You will be astounded by the wonders awaiting you there."

I close my eyes and once again step through the carved gate into the evolving paradise of my imagination. I'm swept into the magic of this resplendent place. From my pavilion, I can see how much territory is opening up around me.

Chinese Medicine is there beside me, and I hear her say, "This is where it begins. As your tranquility deepens, the inspired brilliance of Heaven and the sweet sensuality of Earth integrate within you. You become luminosity and ecstasy entwined. Your capacity to embody love encircles you and stretches into all moments. This is your future becoming present, your true self returning to the sanctuary of your heart. It is the Way."

Chinese Medicine Seeds of Transformation

❷ My heart is where my home is.

❷ I am a temple of miracles.

❷ I am a living altar of soul and cells.

❷ I am a love child of Heaven and Earth.

❷ I am angel and animal entwined.

❷ My creative genius illuminates my cellular structure.

❷ My heart is the sanctuary of Heaven and Earth and the home of my true self.

❷ The voices of my senses are crystal clear, guiding me always to more joy.

❷ I am the creative conduit of Heaven and Earth.

❷ My body is Heaven's feet, and my spirit, Earth's wings.

☯ I take pleasure in each step of my journey.

☯ I weave pleasure into my everyday life.

☯ I honor my body and spirit as equals.

☯ I embody the natural grace of *being* a human being.

☯ I am an ever-flowing font of creativity.

☯ I am generous with the gift of time.

☯ I am life enjoying itself.

☯ I am life, loving life.

☯ I celebrate the ever-unfolding love affair of my spirit and flesh.

☯ My imagination soars, gathers what was once unimaginable, and returns ecstatic.

☯ I invite my creative genius to shape every moment.

☯ I pay kind attention to my inner and outer worlds and fully express who I am.

❷ I kiss the past and let it go.

❷ I live in an ever-evolving paradise of my own making.

❷ On the wings of my imagination, I ride the currents of feeling into my inner world.

❷ I imagine my ever-evolving paradise into being.

❷ I fill the sanctuary within my heart with love, love, and more love.

❷ As I breathe life into my inner world, it takes on a vitality of its own and breathes life back into me.

❷ The inspired brilliance of Heaven and the sweet sensuality of Earth merge within me.

❷ I am luminosity and ecstasy entwined.

❷ My capacity to embody love encircles me and stretches into all moments.

The Dance of Stillness and Motion
(*Courtesy Terah Kathryn Collins*)

CHAPTER TWO

Love lives here
In the embodying of kindness

Heart and mind as beloveds
Free the true self

Currents of pleasure and guidance
Become the dance

I Ching stands at the edge of the same circle where Chi-nese Medicine and I sat together, the sleeves of her ivory robe trailing fluidly to the floor. Her hair is bound in a smooth chignon held by a slender mother-of-pearl wand.

She gracefully lifts her arm, and her sleeve arcs through the air in a silken flash. It drifts out across the circle and softly lands, dividing the space in half with a flowing line. She's still for a moment, then draws her arm back, her sleeve lifting like a sinuous ribbon and returning to her side. A clear impression of the flowing line remains.

She then moves into one side of the circle and nods to me, a greeting. I spontaneously return the gesture. She closes her eyes and becomes completely motionless, her alabaster hands resting on her heart.

I Ching remains still for several moments, then moves to the other side of the circle. She begins to whirl, her dance building into a mesmerizing sweep and flow of graceful improvisations. She's a rushing river, a leaping animal, a leaf turning in the wind. She weaves her way around the circle several times, dancing on one side, not moving on the other, going from free-form expression to deep repose, a revolving portrayal of stillness and motion.

She finishes in the center of the circle and faces me, beckoning me to join her with a subtle nod. I step into the circle, feeling her amber eyes focused fully upon me. They mean business.

"Your journey home continues," she says, her voice strong and absolute. "Chinese Medicine's poetic descriptions of the Way helped you begin to actually *feel* your true nature. She has warmed you up for me. You've moved past the numb phase and glimpsed some of what is possible. You've felt the first stirrings of light in your body, reclaimed the

20

wings of your imagination, and begun to explore your inner world."

She steps closer to me, her gaze intensifying, "Basically, you're pointed in the right direction, and you still have a lot of work to do. You were taught to worship your mind and ignore your heart, depraving one and depriving the other. Any loving feelings you may have are immediately imprisoned by harsh judgments and refused expression. Your true self cannot live in such caustic conditions."

I picture a dismal medieval prison where women are jailed, while men clomp around in heavy armor.

"Your imagery is symbolically accurate," I Ching says. "When your thoughts override your feelings, harmony is lost. The Way knows no such hierarchy. It is your true nature to appreciate your mind and heart, your body and spirit, animals and people, angels and atoms, everyone and everything as essentially equal, all with their unique gifts to give." She stretches out her arms and stamps both feet. "It is all equal!"

Struck by her fervor, I stretch my arms and stamp my feet, too, repeating, "Equal!"

"Yes! Your life transforms when you stop dissecting everything and labeling the pieces as more or less deserving of dignity and care. What a waste of time and energy that is, when you can simply cherish all of Creation as it exists. The Way is inclusive, not exclusive. Your heart and mind are meant to be lovers, not enemies. Like Heaven and Earth, they wish only to live as equals in harmony within you. It's their kind wisdom together, the sublime flow of their discerning devotion, that creates the loving world where you—the true you—can thrive."

Goose bumps of truth run up and down my spine. I know she's right.

I Ching assesses me and says, "That jail you just saw is real, you know. You walk around in it every day; you wake up in it, toss and turn in the middle of the night in it, and relate to people in it. You live there because you keep choosing to think, speak, and act as though your feelings don't matter. Stop doing that! Such hierarchical choices are abusive, and they make your life a prison rather than a paradise. The Way is paved with loving-kindness—the essence of your heart and mind, your spirit and flesh, every inner and outer part of you . . . flowing together as equals in the dance of harmony."

She pauses, letting me absorb her words, then continues: "Because you shape your world one thought, word, and deed at a time, you must choose every moment to be kind to yourself and others. Although it may seem laborious at first, it's imperative." She steps even closer and whispers emphatically, "Kindness reveals the Way. It's how you find the path home."

Her words are so simple, yet their meaning sends a bolt of recognition through me. Of course it's how I find my way home. I flush from head to toe as I begin to actually feel what it would be like to live in a kind and caring world.

"Good—let your feelings and thoughts intertwine. Feel and imagine what it's like to be surrounded by love in a world steeped in kindheartedness."

Feeling and imagining so much is overwhelming. In fact, I feel as if I'm going to faint.

"Come here," I Ching says. She puts her arms around me, and I melt into her. Memories of so much unkindness pour through me. She holds me steady as I ride a flood of emotions into a whole new world of possibilities.

"Help is always with you," she says softly.

I feel the sting of my own sarcastic thoughts: *What help? I've survived by being alone.*

She stands back, fixing me in her fierce gaze. "Alone and always in your head is how you endured the past. It's also why your heart is opening at a glacial pace. Your worldview says aloof isolation is required for survival. Not so. To find your way home, you must transform your feral habits. The truth is that you're not alone; and you're not meant to spend all your time in your head, especially with thoughts that are so . . ." I Ching pauses, appraising me for a moment, ". . . punishing.

"Use those newfound wings of yours and imagine this." She waits for me to close my eyes, then continues, "Visualize yourself walking down a hallway and opening a long line of locked doors as you go. With every one you unlock, you set free another loving feeling. Imagine each feeling returning to your heart like a spark of light, your whole body becoming more illuminated with every door you unseal."

I see heavy doors swing open. Beautiful orbs of light race toward my chest, making a beeline for home. One light after another illuminates my heart, a true housewarming.

Darkness evaporates; and paradise expands all around me, my inner sanctuary becoming more vividly real than ever before.

"Light and space are dawning within you," says I Ching as I open my eyes. She smiles briefly, and then becomes serious again. "And don't fool yourself—you're just beginning and are far from done. You'll have opportunities every day to open more doors and free other parts of your true nature. You must stay with it, dedicate yourself to this work, and call yourself back to it over and over again. Feel, think, speak, and act loving-kindness into being. Practice, practice, practice until you're fluent."

She brings her hands to her hips, her sleeves pooling on the floor around her. "One of your most powerful tools is language. With it, you can kiss or kill your progress. Words are meant to express love, not destroy it. It's impossible to open your heart when you're engaged in killing with thoughts or words. When you choose language that acts as a potion rather than a poison, you're opening yourself to the pleasure, brilliance, and grace of life."

I feel her voice as notes of truth, playing through me. It pulls me where I haven't been before.

"As you choose words to 'kiss' the world around you, you call a new reality into being. You find that the benevolence of your chosen vocabulary is mirrored in your outer world, and you become enchanted by the continuum of kindness flowing through your everyday life. As you weave love and compassion into the auditory fabric of your days, you experience them circling around and returning the kiss. You feel them brushing against your skin. Your thoughts and words can be portals through which Heaven on Earth manifests."

A hint of a smile crosses her face as she continues, "Life is so much more enjoyable when you focus on the blessings rather than the challenges. Every moment can be like improvisational theater, where you take great pleasure in either observing or participating in each unique scene. People; places; things; and the spontaneous arrangement of words, patterns, colors, sounds, tastes, scents, and feelings portray Creation in constant motion. No two seconds are exactly alike. You can sit back and watch the show or jump in, whatever suits you in the moment."

I flash on a recent trip to the grocery store. Standing in line, I become aware of the unique collage of people, items on the conveyor belt, music, and machines around me. A tabloid headline: "Tempted by Another Woman," oversees purchases of cat food and cheese sticks to the tune of "Satisfaction," which is playing over the sound system. The scanner chimes while the woman in front of me slides her credit card, swings her baby away from the candy, and answers her cell phone—all in one smooth motion. She moves like a synchronized swimmer, breaststroking child, phone, and cart out of the store. The fleeting beauty of the scene strikes me as an original work of art in motion, there and gone, another unique moment rising up like a wave around me.

"You slipped into sync with the heartbeat of Creation," I Ching comments. "You found your front-row seat and let life sweep you up in its arms and dance with you. Enough of those types of moments and you know what's going to happen?" She smiles knowingly. "You're going to really start enjoying yourself."

Clearly, I've missed a lot of enjoyment along the Way.

"You didn't know that pleasure and kindness are your partners in life," she replies. "Now you do, so no more excuses. And you always have your imagination, which is already beginning to serve you well. You're meant to relish every opportunity to flow in and out of the seen and unseen worlds. You've only just begun to explore and delight in your nonphysical existence."

I Ching studies me and says, "Your sanctuary exists within the vast territory of your inner world, you know. You have so much more to discover. Go there often and explore to your heart's content. The wings of your imagination and your capacity to create are strengthened with each journey you take."

I recall a recent daydream in an airport, imagining everyone waltzing around the luggage carousel, the tedium of waiting transformed into a whirling dance.

"Yes, that's a perfect example. You're meant to love your life, not be miserably entrapped by it. It can be as good as you're able to imagine."

She takes my hand and says, "Come walk with me," directing me over to the half of the circle where she'd been so still.

She lets go of my hand, steps close, and whispers, "You must learn to be quiet! You require silence to commune with and be nurtured by the unseen world. Your lopsided lifestyle has all but excluded this vital connection, depriving you of so much of your potential. You think you live alone in the dark because your eyes are closed. You're in for some very pleasant surprises when you open your eyes and see who and what surrounds you."

An almost-palpable stillness enfolds us for several moments before she speaks again. "The union of your heart and mind is illuminated by silence. In the quiet, you can clearly feel and articulate your inner truth. You can take deep pleasure in the evolving marvels of your entire nonphysical world." She pauses, her face full of light. "You can also ask the helpers who walk beside you to do whatever is necessary to bring any situation—any part of your life—back into balance."

I lean toward her as I remember Chinese Medicine's mention of inner helpers.

"Yes," I Ching continues, "now that you have an inner place, you can get to know your inner friends. In the past, you learned that you must beg for help from higher beings who considered you inferior. Instead of groveling, however, you rejected the notion of the unseen world as being superior and ventured forth alone. Neither is the Way. You're meant to reach *in* for help, not *up*, and travel through life with an internal entourage of loving helpers who are best described as friends. They have the same wonderful qualities as the people you consider your closest companions. Even in the dark cacophony of your past when they were like strangers to you, these unseen partners helped you."

A vivid memory flashes through my mind. I'm 21 and hitchhiking from Phoenix to Tucson. The man who picks me up immediately pulls out a gun and takes the next exit. I watch his hand remove the gun from the glove box in front of me, feel the slowing of the car, and hear an inner voice say, *When you get to the gravel road, open the door and jump out.*

It never occurs to me to question the voice, and I never look at the man again. The exit ramp leads to a gravel road, the car slows to about 30 miles an hour, and I open the door and jump out. I hit the gravel and am up and running toward the only thing around—a mobile construction office—as the man makes a U-turn and speeds back to the highway. Then I'm falling through the construction workers' door in search of help. I don't hear the inner voice again as I make my way to the hospital with a remarkable lack of injuries. I need stitches in several places, and a hundred pieces of gravel are embedded under my skin, but I'm well enough to hear the doctor's lecture on how lucky I am to be alive.

I Ching shakes her head. "You've certainly been a handful. Throughout all your difficulties, your unseen friends have done their best to help you along the Way."

I wonder about this. I've felt an occasional sense of being supported throughout the years, especially when things weren't going well. I hadn't experienced this mysterious assistance as coming from friendly companions, though. I'd always assumed unseen help intermittently came from beings that might hang around more if I was willing to beg—friends indeed.

"You recognized that those in the unseen world aren't superior, but you believed they offered you no loving support. The truth is that they've always carefully watched over you. So much of your anxiety has come from thinking that you were alone and had to solve every challenge by yourself. The raw clench of anxiety, anger, or fear is meant to signal you to *ask for help,* not push you deeper into the dark maze of anguish. When you discern that there's *anything* out of balance, turn within and ask for help. This is true for every kind of distress, from the smallest personal concerns to the greatest collective dilemmas."

Some dark wall disintegrates within me. On the other side is an expanse of rolling hills in every shade of green, with everything bathed in sunlight.

"Good," I Ching says. "Another piece of your prison wall just came down. It's time you saw the forever view on the other side. Knowing you're not here to solve all of life's challenges by yourself transforms anxiety into acceptance. The Way is familial, not feudal. You realize how interdependent you are with all of Creation, offer your assistance whenever you can, and humbly ask for help when you need it. This is how the circle of loving-kindness is sustained."

She stands completely still, gathering her thoughts. "The most challenging time to ask for help is the first time. The next most difficult is the second time, and so on. Your trust in your inner helpers can only be built through familiarity, and silence is where they reside. When you take the time to commune with them, you discover you're never alone. You surrender to the loving guidance they've always offered you.

"You must cultivate your relationship with them. Sit quietly and ask them to join you in your inner sanctuary. Invite them in for tea. Ask for their assistance and support as you would ask your dear friends. Listen to them, let them inspire and delight you, and most of all . . . ," she touches my hands, ". . . *feel* how much they love you."

I sense the enormity of her words reshaping every part of my being. Even when I'm physically alone, loving beings surround me. I imagine having tea with angels, sharing cups of kindness in my garden pavilion.

"Your inner helpers can appear as angels, animals, people you do or don't know, orbs of light, nature spirits, flowers, trees—you name it." I Ching pauses while I absorb her words, then suggests, "You can learn a lot about them by contemplating the qualities you love in your most cherished friends and family members. What attracts you to them?"

She watches me as I consider her question. I think of my favorite people and realize they have many similar attributes. I seem to prize playfulness, honesty, kindness, joy, creativity, and generosity. My closest friends are inspiring, optimistic, and great fun to be with.

"There you go." She smiles and winks, surprising me. "All those qualities describe your nonphysical friends as well. They, too, are benevolent, playful beings—just like the people you adore."

Having so many new friends makes me wonder about my dreams. They're full of people and animals I don't know in my waking life.

"Helpers, all of them," I Ching answers, as I recall a vivid dream from many years ago. A young man with long brown hair is facing me, standing very close. He shouts, "Your name is Terah!" so loud that it awakens me with a jolt at 3 A.M. The next day, I happen upon the spelling in *The Aquarian Gospel of Jesus the Christ;* and struck by the synchronicity, I change my name from Kathryn Louise to Terah Kathryn.

"Yes, the man in your dream has assisted you many times," I Ching says, amber light sparkling in her eyes. "The unseen world is quite fluid. Helpers manifest according to the needs of the moment. Some are with you for a lifetime, some just for a day or a moment. They each have their unique contributions to make, just as all beings in the seen world do. No concern is too great or too small.

"There are unseen helpers to save your life, instruct you in the language of kindness, heal your body and the planet, inspire your work, ignite your imagination, find answers to life's conundrums, direct you to the right places and people at the right time, protect you, love you, and guide you home. All you have to do is ask for their aid and be thankful when you receive it. When anything distressing occurs, ask for help to do whatever is necessary to balance the situation; then feel grateful for the loving assistance that surrounds you, and let it go."

I picture an overgrown garden where several people are clearing weeds. Their work reveals bountiful flowers and trees, the grounds taking on a lush symmetry as the beauty of the original design becomes more and more evident.

"The garden of your true self is being restored," I Ching observes. "The weeds of heartlessness that once choked you are being removed. Your true nature has always been there, hidden beneath layers of troublesome conditioning. Now, your unseen friends are helping you return to your full magnificence."

She studies me and I feel new warmth pouring from her. Her voice is soothing. "You're learning that you aren't supposed to do it all yourself. You're here to be the creative conduit of Heaven and Earth, as Chinese Medicine likes to say, and to blossom and grow in the great mystery of life. When you can *feel* the pure wonder of the inner and outer realms coursing together through your veins, you're in sync with the majesty of life. Deeply engaged, you become a cascade of gratitude, a font of appreciation for the majesty of life pouring through you."

She takes my hand, and we move to the center of the circle. She turns to me and says, "You're rekindling the sacred union of your heart and mind and restoring your connection with all of creation. As you remember your native tongue and become fluent in the language of kindness, your true self can fully emerge and enjoy life's eternal improvisations. You're opening to the heavenly world of your unseen friends and becoming supple in the ways of love. . . . Now, we shall dance."

I have no idea what to expect. Will I waltz with her around the circle? No, this is going to be something new.

"Yes, new and also timeless. Dance lives in every cell of your body, innate rhythms all humans share. When love is dancing through you, you embody the choreography of your true self and gracefully move to the rhythm of your inner knowing and outer circumstances. Because they're always changing, you fluidly improvise. You recognize when to lead or follow, give or receive, speak or listen, depending upon the moment. You glide and swirl, pause and turn, flowing in sync with the Way."

I can feel it. My desire to connect with other hearts ripples out and blends with the deep fulfillment of sharing life's blessings with my kindred spirits. I imagine communing with my beloved, our closeness blurring the line between us, rapture building. . . .

"You're blushing," I Ching observes. "And yes, pleasure is always looking for ways to move through you. The energy of creation flows like ecstasy through your body, your temple of miracles resonating with the current of life."

Various pleasures spring to mind—the verdant embrace of the garden; velvety hummingbirds in aerial ballet; the blue jay's warm feet as she lands in my hand; and sunsets on the beach, bundled in a coat and blanket, happy to disappear into the oceanic wonder. I think of my magical friends and our conversations; repasts; and most of all, our deepening sense of belonging, a constant stream of love weaving us together. Something opens within me. I can no longer hold these moments as simple or small. They are, every one, profound.

"Your true self knows no ordinary moments," I Ching murmurs. "Every one is extraordinary."

She looks at me and asks softly, "Do you feel the presence of unseen friends in the circle?"

I instantly do. I feel shy, as though I'm reuniting with long-lost family. I'm sure my grandmother is there, the scent of roses and hot chocolate perfuming the air. I catch glimpses of the man from my naming dream and other benevolent presences around the circle.

I Ching watches me closely and asks, "Can you see the gift they bring you?"

My grandmother seems to be holding something in her hands. I soften my gaze and let it come to me. It's luminous, shaped like a heart. I think, *If I could have a heart like that, I could be my true self again.*

I Ching stands poised in her ivory robe. "You can. You're fully merging with the dance of physical and non-physical life. Now it's time to feel it stream through your body." She curtsies low, pure grace in motion; and I long to move as she does.

"I move from the inside out," she says. "And so can you. You're a channel of love between two worlds, your body a somatic treasure whose joy is to dance with life."

She steps into the side of the circle where she moved so beautifully and whirls slowly around. "Every moment of life is meant to engage and inspire you. Let your movements flow spontaneously from within, as *being* rather than *doing*."

She reaches up and slowly removes the mother-of-pearl wand from her chignon, her long, raven hair tumbling down her back. Tucking the wand into her sash, she looks into my eyes and brings her hands to her heart, her movements light and unhurried. I mirror her, feeling a rush of energy stream through my body. She extends her hands toward me, palms softly facing me, and I do the same. We touch, and I'm suffused with warmth. A magnetic pull flowers between us. Holding my gaze, she slowly brings her hands back to her heart and whispers, "Become the dance."

I'm still for a moment as feelings bubble to the surface. I watch her begin to move with greater abandon—her arms spread wide, hair and sleeves flowing like silken poetry around her—a whirling flash of turns and bends. Her passion astonishes me, grace gone wild and contagious. I surrender, ecstasy running through me. I yield to the sweep of my body and am transported. I am the dance dancing, the circle of love turning. I'm the pulse of my own blood, washing the elixir of exaltation through every cell of my being.

Then I'm still, my heart luminous. There it is.

I Ching looks at me, her face radiant. "Your heart returns to you—and this time you know how to keep it."

I Ching Seeds
of Transformation

- My mind, heart, body, and spirit each contribute unique gifts to my life.

- My thoughts and feelings live in harmony with each other.

- My heart and mind are lovers.

- I embody love, compassion, and kindness.

- I infuse love, compassion, and kindness into my thoughts, words, and actions.

- Paradise manifests all around me.

- Pleasure and kindness are my guiding lights.

- I relish every opportunity to expand my creative genius.

- I let my imagination soar.

- I have an inner entourage of loving helpers who are my friends.

- ☯ Every cell of my body is illuminated, animated, and sustained by my nonphysical helpers.

- ☯ I am embraced in a Circle of Belonging.

- ☯ I am always guided to the right places and people at the right time.

- ☯ I am open to receiving help from my unseen friends.

- ☯ I am constantly protected and loved by my nonphysical friends.

- ☯ My true nature blossoms in its full magnificence.

- ☯ The inner and outer realms course equally through my veins.

- ☯ I fully embody my true self.

- ☯ I am a cascade of gratitude and a font of appreciation.

- ☯ The majesty of life pours through me.

- ☯ I am supple in the ways of love.

☯ Love dances through me.

☯ I embody the choreography of my true self
and gracefully move to the rhythm of my inner
knowing and outer circumstances.

☯ I fluidly improvise and recognize when to lead or
follow, give or receive, and speak or listen.

☯ I glide and swirl, pause and turn, flowing in sync
with the Way.

☯ I enjoy the deep fulfillment of sharing blessings
with my circle of kindred spirits.

☯ The ecstasy of life flows through my body.

☯ Every moment is extraordinary.

☯ I merge with the full circle of my physical and
nonphysical life.

☯ I am a channel of love between two worlds.

☯ My body is a somatic treasure whose joy is to
dance with life.

☯ I am the dance dancing, the circle of love turning.

☯ I am the pulse of my own blood, washing the elixir of exaltation through every cell of my being.

☯ My heart is luminous.

The Embrace of Yin and Yang
(Courtesy Terah Kathryn Collins)

CHAPTER THREE

Love lives here
In waves of harmony

Affinity of person and place
Illuminates the true self

Undulating resonance
Completes the circle

Feng Shui busily paints one side of the circle black. Following the impression made by the sleeve of I Ching's robe, the other side is already painted pure white. Each part contains a large dot of the opposite color. She looks up and smiles, waving me into the white half of the circle.

"That side is already dry," she says, her effervescence pulling me in. Her long braid slides across the back of her embroidered robe as she finishes her work. She has the poise and grace of her Sisters, with a lightness of being all her own.

"Do you remember moving with I Ching here in the circle?" she asks, amethyst eyes twinkling.

"I do," I murmur, a wave of pleasure accompanying the memory.

"Yes, she's quite a dancer. She taught me how to dance, too . . . and how to think, speak, be kind, listen to my true self, and ask for assistance from my unseen helpers," she says in a singsong manner, moving her head from side to side. "She's always teaching me something!

"Chinese Medicine is the quiet one in the family. She has taught me so much without saying a word. She used to take me into the garden when I was a baby and put me in a cradle hung in a willow tree. I can still remember how safe and warm I felt, swinging gently in the breeze, reaching for the birds . . . there were always so many birds."

I picture the scene, feeling the sweetness of it. I imagine myself in the cradle, looking up at the blue sky and frolicking birds, rocking warm and weightless in the leafy shade.

"Your desire to live in harmony opens you to transformation," Feng Shui says, beaming at me. "You're discovering that everything is alive in your environment; and as you do, your whole world is changing. You see that all buildings are essentially living beings with a noble purpose, born to be safe havens along the Way."

She stops for a moment, her smile fading. "Your environment is a mirror, you know. It reflects the harmony or discord in your life. Fortunately," her smile returns, "even in the most discordant circumstances and conditions, love and harmony can be restored. No matter how deeply buried the treasures of life are, you can find them again. It is the Way."

Feng Shui checks her black paint, now dry, and motions me over to a stack of silk cushions. "Choose your favorite," she suggests. I select a shimmering turquoise pillow, while she chooses one in deep crimson; and we settle in the middle of the circle.

"Transforming your life begins with a shift in perception about yourself and your surroundings." She takes my hands, squeezing them affectionately. "It begins with imagining the whole environment, natural and human-made, as a continuum of love, encompassing the entire planet and beyond; all of it as inspiring, healing, and blessed as the structures and landscapes you call sacred sites."

Stonehenge springs to mind. I can still sense the ripples of energy surging from the ancient circle of stones.

"That's the feeling! It's the rhythmic wash of resonant energy, circling out and bathing everything. Many people travel the globe in search of the harmonious energies found in certain special places. They seek to quench their thirst for Heaven on Earth by drinking from a rare font, when all the while a sacred well remains untapped at home." She touches her heart with both hands. "It all begins with your open-heartedness moving out through your body, your home, and beyond. When you feel the continuum of love, you discover that the Way isn't just randomly dotted with the sacred; it's infused with it.

"This is how it flows," she says, making a circle with her delicate hands. "Your true self lives in your heart, your heart lives in your body, your body lives in your home, your home lives in your community, your community lives in your country, your country lives on your planet, and out and out it goes." She makes bigger and bigger circles as she talks, until her arms are stretched as wide as possible. "Just imagine your Circle of Belonging interconnecting with other circles, every heart open; every home, city, and country sending out and receiving resonant waves of love."

I breathe this in. I imagine vibrant rings of energy flowing out from every person and building, touching and blending with each other; continuing out through great tracts of farmland, wilderness, cities, towns, and beyond. The effect is like endless ripples intermingling and spreading across a clear lake.

"The patterns in Nature are always showing us the Way. When love flows freely, all beings thrive. You can feel the flow, right here and now." Her voice plays through me. We look into each other's eyes, and she holds her hands out to me. I take them, our connection quickening my pulse.

"Doesn't that feel good?" she asks, closing her eyes and inhaling deeply.

Yes, it does. A warm current flows into my left palm, through my body, and out my right palm into hers. The energy builds and deepens; and I feel it circulating through every cell, my heart brightening, expanding. Circles of energy intensify around us, rippling out with every breath.

"This is how love feels," Feng Shui murmurs, "a constant symphony of resonance circulating within and around you."

She opens her eyes and gently lets go of my hands. I'm suffused with warmth, grounded and euphoric at the same time. She smiles brightly.

"The truth is, love is all you're really interested in. As you discovered with my Sisters, it opens many pathways of pleasure in your being. Everything they shared with you about your inner world ripples out to include the things surrounding you in the outer world. When your environment reflects who you truly are, it completes the circle of the seen and unseen realms. Your environment becomes a continuum of love. Isn't that wonderful?"

It *is* wonderful—and it makes me consider what I love in my surroundings. I immediately think of the painting I see when I wake up every morning.

"It says, 'Yes!' whenever you see it or think of it, doesn't it?" Feng Shui asks, nodding her head. "What about the painting makes your heart sing?"

I pause to contemplate this. There's a haunting quality about it that sweeps me into untouched wilderness. Sandstone cliffs above a pale blue sea, windswept green headlands, an arched rock bridging land with mossy islands . . . all pull me into another world. Sky meets sea in the distance, a forever view calling me to wonder and wander. There, I am free.

"Beloved belongings reflect and affirm who you are. They nurture your true self. There's a reason they're called *belongings*—you belong together. Your painting echoes your own voice, saying, 'I cherish my freedom and the beauty of Nature.' It calls you into your fullness every morning. Imagine having such a loving relationship with everything in your surroundings, a choir of harmonious voices all around you."

I'd love to hear them sing. Both as a child and an adult, I've often been told that it didn't matter what I loved—I was lucky to get whatever I got, usually on sale. People with preferences were often called picky and spoiled. When I came to realize my personal desires were essential in deciphering what nurtured and sustained me, I looked through magazines and catalogs and collected pictures of spaces and things I found especially attractive. I noticed I was drawn to certain colors, styles, and moods over and over again. My collection showed eclectic spaces comprising oriental, rustic, and outdoorsy elements. Turquoise and golden tones predominated in intimate cozy spaces that were cast in natural light. I could hear the beautiful voices of my true preferences, and they really did make my heart sing.

"Notice how you're feeling," Feng Shui suggests.

I feel exhilarated, the vital connection between home and heart filling me with new energy.

"Let's keep going!" she exclaims with a big smile. "What else do you love?"

I immediately think of two lamps I adore, both heirlooms from my maternal grandmother. One is made from a tall oriental vase of fine porcelain, awarded to my great-grandfather for his culinary expertise as a chef. Grandmom had it made into a lamp, and I remember it as one of her most beautiful possessions. She gave it to me 30 years ago, along with another lamp crafted by her husband, my grandfather. Originally a wedge of cedar fence post, he intricately carved the golden wood with doves; flowers; and a woman in a long, flowing dress. Although I never met either man, I feel the essence of their creative spirits is kept illuminated by the lamps. To me, they're living treasures.

Feng Shui reaches out to me and says, "Both lamps carry the legacy of your relatives' creative genius, an inheritance you deeply cherish. No matter what the origin of our possessions, even when they're heirlooms or considered valuable in some way, it's vital to check the resonance factor. Ideally, everything is saying, 'Yes, yes, yes!'"

She looks at me inquisitively and asks, "Why did your grandmother give you the lamps?"

Because she knew how much I love them, I muse. I remember the day she gave them to me. She was moving into an assisted-living facility and had no room for the lamps. I can still feel the poignancy of her passing her beloved symbols of father and husband on to me. She knew how I felt about them, and put them into my safekeeping.

"She found a good home for the precious things she could no longer provide shelter for," Feng Shui says softly. "There's a time when all things move on, even the ones you love. When those times come, it is the Way to find them a good home. Your grandmother did well, and someday you will do the same."

Her words and the memory of my grandmother fill me with a profound sense of gratitude. As tangibles, the lamps hold the intangible in place. The past benevolently lives with me and carries me into the future, embraced in the harmonious atmosphere that time and love create together.

"On the other hand," Feng Shui says, snapping her fingers around her, "disliked or disorganized things create a very different atmosphere. Listen and you can hear their complaints and grievances flying through the air."

I immediately hear the quibbling of two oak chairs. *Why are they in my life?* I wonder. Long ago, a roommate gave them to me when she moved out of our shared apartment. I've kept them as spare seating because they're high-quality, solid oak, even though I've never liked how they feel on my back.

"Ah, so the chairs aren't comfortable," Feng Shui observes. "Comfort and safety are the guardians of your personal well-being. The high quality of materials doesn't matter when they don't feel good to you. Although you may encounter unsafe, uncomfortable conditions out in the world, your home is meant to be your sanctuary."

She takes my hands again, wishing to make a point. "Despite all your knowledge of arranging spaces to be aesthetically pleasing, this is new for you. As you step fully into your true self, anything you're out of tune with becomes obvious. You'll find that it's easy and natural to let go of the things you don't resonate with and surround yourself with what comforts, pleases, and inspires you."

She leans in closer. "This is fun. Imagine comfort as the mother, and safety as the father. Beauty is their precocious child. Safety steers you away from things with sharp corners or other dangerous features. He lights dark places so that you can always find your way. Comfort embraces and nourishes you with favorite textures, colors, scents, flavors, and sounds. As discerning parents, they guide Beauty in making wise choices. A beautiful anything—whether it's a chair, table, or bed—can only serve you well when it's also safe and comfortable."

I'm already planning to donate the chairs to the local resource center.

"Perfect!" Feng Shui squeezes my hands and lets them go. "Bless them and let them move on to their new home. Everyone will be happier—you and the chairs."

I mentally scan my surroundings, sorting through my belongings for more discordant voices. A coffee mug, given to me by a former boyfriend, grumbles in the cupboard. I realize that I think of him every day when I see that mug. He's practically living with me.

"He *is* living with you!" Feng Shui says, nudging my arm to make her point. "You have daily contact with him via the mug. If you treasure the memories of him, great; if you don't, give it away along with the chairs."

Treasure the memories? No, quite the opposite—I'd rather not recall those unhappy times every day. I'm looking forward to ushering his mug out of the house as soon as possible.

"The sooner, the better is right." Feng Shui watches me intently. "Ideally, your environment contains the things you currently love. Treasure the belongings that hold wonderful memories and uplifting feelings in place, and let go of what doesn't. Let safety, comfort, and beauty be your guides. And know in your heart that your responses to the things in your surroundings may change as you evolve. What you love today, you may not care for or have space for tomorrow."

Whoa! Now I'm spinning. The kindness in her face steadies me.

"Feel the freedom in this. When you tune in to the voices of your possessions, you know whether they're affirming you or not. The things 'who' lend a beautiful voice to your environmental choir are welcome to stay. As time passes, certain members of your chorus fall out of harmony, a sign they're ready to move on. Bless them, thank them, and let them go. Can you feel what a difference this makes in the quality of your life?"

It's the difference between living with a blessing or a curse. Suddenly, I can feel how burdensome it is to be with things I don't have a loving connection with.

"Burdensome to both you *and* the objects," Feng Shui says. "Extend your practice of kindness to every item living with you. The kindest thing you can do is to let possessions you don't love or need return to the flow. Honor and appreciate the contributions all things make in the world. Essentially, the coffee mug is no less sacred than your beloved painting; the oak chairs deserve to be treated with the same dignity as your lamps. Because you don't resonate with them, you kindly let them go so that they may continue their journey."

I think of the jumble of stuff in my garage and cringe, knowing what Feng Shui is about to say.

"You know every possession you live with matters! It all counts, just as every one of your thoughts, words, and actions counts. Treat the things in your storage areas with the same tender loving care as everything else, even when you think nobody sees them. You see them, and you are *not* a nobody!"

She gently waves her hands near my face as though she's washing something away. "Remember what I Ching told you. Shift the hierarchical mind-set that insists some things merit better care than others, and level the playing field. Instead of classifying your possessions by a certain pecking order, simply give a good home to everything you love and need; and honor the rest by letting it go. This, more than anything, strengthens the continuum of love and harmony in your life."

Her face becomes stern, reminding me of I Ching. "The things in your garage are in chaos because nothing has a good home. You also have stuff in there you'll never need or use. As it is, the squalid conditions in your garage cause you to feel irritated, confused, and overwhelmed, creating daily dissonance within you." She leans toward me and shakes her head. "Don't derail yourself like that!"

Something clicks. I don't have 25 cats because I can't give 25 cats a good home.

"Exactly—a perfect analogy. Too much of anything compromises everything. When you let go of excessive possessions and focus on creating a good home for those things you love and wish to live with, your environment becomes a symphony of blessings."

Feng Shui touches my hands and says, "Once you've brought your surroundings into resonant order, the energy really gets going, and guess what happens?" She pauses, excitement lighting her face. "Your true self goes wild! With your inner and outer worlds aligned, you become a flowing font of creativity; and your environment becomes one of your favorite playgrounds."

Her words remind me of how my neighbors turned their living room into a video studio, a conversion that lasted several months while they made a holiday video. With black velvet on the windows, sound equipment, lights, and cameras all around, it thrilled me to see their space sheltering so much potent creativity. They paid no attention to all the rules about how living rooms are supposed to look and turned it into a one-of-a-kind beehive of artistic activity.

Feng Shui grins with delight. "I love when that happens! They were expressing their inner directives rather than following outer dictates. A home is meant to sing the songs of the people who live there, the original music inspired by their unique interpretations of life. Your creativity is the signature of Heaven and Earth, you know. When it comes calling, let it in!

"Many people treat their creative spirits like formal wear hanging in the back of a closet, worn only on special occasions. It's time to let go of the formalities and wear your creativity every day. A steady stream of such expression breathes vitality into you and your surroundings. It engages you in the magic of the moment, where the opportunities to be innovative are always emerging."

Her expression changes, becoming serious again. "Hierarchical mind-sets attempt to arrange things vertically, from most to least important. You've done this with the various parts of your home. No area is less deserving of care than another." She raises an eyebrow. "Like your garage, for instance. When some areas are neglected while others are lavished with attention, harmony is lost in the grinding imbalance. Each room and space in your home serves a unique function, much like the organs in your body. Treat every square inch with the same dignity, knowing that together they all form the living body of your home."

She motions around her, hands like small doves. "The circle we're sitting in symbolizes the cyclical movement of harmony. The white half of the circle is called *yang* and represents many aspects of life, including day, sun, heat, Heaven, the unseen world, movement, and activity. The black half is called *yin* and symbolizes night, moon, coolness, Earth, the seen world, silence, and stillness. As complementary polarities, they're entirely equal and comprise one harmonious circle of life.

"Imagine the circle always revolving, like a ball in motion." Feng Shui circles her hands in the air as though she's turning a globe. "Yang becomes yin, and yin becomes yang, like the perpetual movement of the days and seasons. Their constant transformation into each other is symbolized by the smaller dots within each half. There's nothing static about the circle of life. Yin and yang signify the eternal revolving movement of all living things.

"You can see Chinese Medicine's trinity of work, play, and rest here. The yang side of the circle is associated with work and productivity, while rest and tranquility are related to the yin side. Play spans both, as the pleasures of your sensuality, vitality, and creativity can be actively yang or quietly yin."

Play . . . I think of how much I love to dance. Slow, fast, yin, yang—I adore it all. Wherever I can, I do.

"Dance is one of your favorite ways to play," she says. "For you, it calls forth the ecstasy of being alive. You can't imagine life without it. Other people experience the same strong magnetic pull toward playing music, creating art, or any special interests and passions that fuel and reflect their true natures. You leave open floor space where someone else would put a table, easel, or piano.

"There can be a hundred identically constructed homes, and no two are alike because the occupants have their unique preferences and lifestyle requirements. When these are fully expressed and celebrated, they generate the rhythmic washes of resonant energy we talked about, circling out as the continuum of love. Can't you just feel it?" she asks, her face glowing.

I glow with her. Yes, I can feel it.

"You and your home share a living partnership. Each abode presents its own possibilities for meeting your needs. Together, you co-create the physical spaces that hold your rest, work, and play in place, assuring your full alignment with the Way.

"Rest can be anchored in any quiet spot, such as a comfortable chair in a private room or alcove—a place where you can retreat from the insistent voices of the computer, exercise equipment, or television. Rest's native habitat is in your bedroom, where the bed reigns and sensual play is invited in like a lover."

I'm intrigued by such an invitation.

Feng Shui smiles and says, "Yes, indeed. Let your playfulness waft gently through the quiet areas and parade boldly through active spaces in the house. Play carries the imaginative surge that can inspire your productivity and deepen your rest." She studies me closely and continues, "You know, the days of restricting your fun-loving spirit are over. Your true self will make sure of that!"

I feel the pleasure of her pronouncement expand my heart.

"No more making work the lord and master of the household. Work can be loud and demanding. It's best given its own dedicated space where you can close a door, sprawl out, and be productive without compromising other areas of the house. Then you can balance and uplift your workspace with playful colors and decor."

I think of the beaded elfin staff, handmade collages, and other favorite mementos I enjoy having in my home office. A variety of music choices sets many moods, including one guaranteed to make me jump out of my chair and dance.

"I love it!" Feng Shui rocks back on her cushion and laughs. "When work gets too ponderous, you know just what to do. And when you really need a break, you can leave it all contained in its own domain. No more paperwork snarling at you from the dining table. With work corralled elsewhere, you can enjoy nourishing food, conversation, or introspection in a dining area enlivened by the art, lighting, and table settings you love.

"Stay open to shifting and changing any part of your surroundings to accurately reflect the newest you," she offers. "As your interests, needs, and preferences evolve, give them a place to live. Stay open to all of the possibilities. Bedrooms may become home offices, formal living rooms can turn into art studios, and basements may become second living spaces. Your home's purpose is to shelter you through all your transformations."

She touches her heart and then motions around her. "As you've experienced here in this circle, harmony begins within you. My Sisters have guided you in revitalizing your true self and restoring the endangered habitat of your heart. You've reclaimed the wings of your imagination and begun to explore the magnitude of your inner frontiers. Your joie de vivre increases exponentially as your inner and outer worlds flow in one harmonious circle."

She pauses and straightens her body, the essence of her Sisters moving through her. "Honor all of who you are. Live with what you love, and let everything else continue its journey. Celebrate your passions and pleasures and give them places to thrive in the paradise of your own making. Cherish the sacred essence in everyone and everything. You're here to experience a continuum of love as vast as you can imagine. It is the Way."

Feng Shui Seeds
of Transformation

☯ I am a continuum of love.

☯ A gentle wash of resonant love surrounds me.

☯ I am surrounded by sacred space.

☯ My Circle of Belonging expands out in every
direction, embracing me in love.

☯ My heart is open.

☯ A symphony of love constantly plays within and
around me.

☯ I surround myself with belongings that comfort,
please, and inspire me.

☯ I honor everything that lives in my home.

☯ I bless the things I do not resonate with and let
them go to continue their journey.

☯ I honor and appreciate the contributions of all
things in the world.

❷ I take loving care of all of my belongings.

❷ My environment is filled with blessings.

❷ I am an ever-flowing font of creativity.

❷ My creativity is the signature of Heaven and Earth. I let it flow.

❷ I celebrate and express my special interests, preferences, and passions in my surroundings.

❷ I fully express my creative genius and fill my surroundings with love and harmony.

❷ I honor all of who I am.

❷ I live with what I love.

❷ I celebrate my passions and pleasures by giving them places to thrive.

❷ I live in the paradise of my own making.

❷ I cherish the sacred essence in everyone and everything.

- My surroundings mirror my true nature.

- I experience a continuum of love as vast as I can imagine.

CHAPTER FOUR

River Eden

Love lives here
In the circle of intimacy

Anima and animus
Compose the true self

Ecstasy's music
Enchants lover and beloved

How have I come to this place of being so pleasured by life? How did I cross the chasm from numbness to enchantment, from loving so little to so much? These questions arise as I sit in the circle with the three Sisters.

"You have been traveling across the chasm far longer than you realize, much of it in the dark of night," Chinese Medicine offers. "You have been dreaming yourself awake since you were born."

I know this is true. My nights are often punctuated with dreams that carry valuable messages into my waking world. A recent one helped me connect with the Sisters.

In my dream, I am in a car with three monks in saffron and burgundy robes. We're all laughing and enjoying the ride up a curvy mountain road. As we reach the top of the mountain, the car leaves the road and flies out into space, plummeting toward a river far below us. I panic and scream, "We're falling!"

The monks are completely calm—smiling, looking ahead, and enjoying the ride. I'm quite taken aback by this. Why aren't they freaking out like I am? Although they say nothing to try to calm me, I follow their example and sit back as the car falls.

When it hits the water, the car disappears, and I'm floating with one of the monks down the river. We bob along until we reach a sandy beach where golden tents are set up for a festival. I'm jubilant, the experience of falling and floating to this beautiful place filling me with wonder.

A woman greets me, and I say, "We just floated here on the river—look, my hair is still wet!" as I run my hands through my dripping locks, and wake up from the dream.

"That was us all right," Feng Shui tells me. "I was the one who floated down the river with you. I Ching was driving."

"I always drive—and I don't know what I'd do without my backseat driver," she says, looking affectionately at Feng Shui. Turning, she studies me for a moment. "We've been in many of your dreams. You remember the ones you're ready to integrate into your life, like that dream about the three monks. We were inviting you to relax and enjoy the ride."

"Many pleasant surprises have wrapped you in their arms as we have journeyed together," Chinese Medicine murmurs, her tone like distant bells. "One in particular."

Indeed. Pleasant surprises began with her astonishing depiction of my heart as a bedchamber for Heaven and Earth. From her tranquil eloquence poured a flow of marvelous images—and feelings. In her own poetic way, she opened me to an inner love affair where my heart became the playground of inspiration and sensuality. In doing so, one pathway of pleasure after another opened within me. Now they're everywhere.

Chinese Medicine smiles softly. "When Heaven and Earth become lovers within you, you see the world through their eyes—opportunities to love life are everywhere. People become welcome playmates; and nature is a feast of beauty, pouring her magic into every moment. A feeling of open-heartedness accompanies every breath. Pleasure, once an occasional outer encounter, now flows steadily within you. Your 'temple of miracles' has opened to fully receive the joy inherent in every moment . . ."

"Which prepared you for me," I Ching declares, her voice pulling me to her. "Chinese Medicine opened the gateways of your authentic self. You've only just begun to experience the pleasures of your true nature. You're claiming the fullness of yourself and embracing the loving help you receive from the unseen world. You're integrating heart and mind, female and male, anima and animus, lover and beloved. You are becoming whole within yourself."

Chills course through my body. So that's what has been going on. I've become acutely aware of a faint whisper, decidedly male, becoming a clear, resonant voice within me. I hear him in my favorite music, the low laugh of a stranger, and the waves tumbling pebbles along the beach. I see him in the smooth curve of a neighbor's jaw and the light-filled eyes of my friends. I smell him on my skin. I feel him in my posture, my libido, and every move I make. He rides in on certain poetry and artwork and pulls me close, provocatively attractive, achingly familiar. I sense him everywhere—my inner beloved, my animus, up close and personal, coming in for a landing.

Feng Shui claps her hands with delight. "Imagine everyone in the whole world having such a juicy experience!"

I Ching looks at me, amused. "Juicy, indeed. All along, you've chosen friends and lovers who offer you a glimpse of he-who-is-you. He reveals himself in all that pleases you. As you've learned to recognize and appreciate him, he shows himself more and more to you. He's a constant presence within you, always reflected in the people and things that turn your head, attract you, and open you to the joys of life. Once, he woke you with his voice and changed the sound of your name. . . ."

A thousand dots connect. His face, so close to mine, many years ago in my naming dream. Of course it was he. I feel his presence more than ever, the meaning of an enigmatic poem I recently wrote becoming crystal clear:

River Eden
I explore you with great interest
A phantom becoming one strong presence
A mystery camping along my wild edges
This is so far what I know
You have always been with me
And you can see in the dark.

"You have opened yourself to him and heard him whisper his name. . . ." Chinese Medicine smiles, the quiet music of her words a warm invitation. "Tell us more about him."

My heart pounds as I recall the slow revealing of him. This is what I know: An alluring poet and dancer with long chestnut hair, he is completely sensual. He's uncharted territory I've just begun to explore as my inner world opens before me. His eyes, the ever-changing color of the sea, look as intimately into mine as I allow, always deepening.

I have only to think of him, and his comforting presence is with me. As my feral numbness dissipates, I feel so much more. When anguish washes over me, I turn to him and draw him close. I hear him say, "It's not that you feel anguish, it's that you *feel!* Your heart experiences all things, and everything is always changing. Emotions are ephemeral butterflies, so transitory and evocative, precious in the world, here briefly to shape your heart and then gone."

He says:

> *You, my beloved*
> *Somehow surviving the world*
> *No longer blossom secretly or alone.*
> *Open your heart,*
> *Surrender to the flow of ecstasy,*
> *And come dance with me.*
>
> *A procession of wild enchantments*
> *Weaves our timeless tendrils together.*
> *Sip from my cup*
> *And I shall sip from yours*
> *An elixir of the heart*
> *Infused with Heaven and Earth.*
>
> *Ride bareback with me into eternity,*
> *Every moment sweet with its own essence*
> *Plucked like miracles*
> *From the field of mystery.*
> *I know where we are going*
> *And it is into forever . . .*

I Ching watches me and says, "All of who he is, you are. He's the inner side of your true self, riding in on the pathways you've opened within. He's joining you again, transforming the archetypal union of Heaven and Earth into an intimate affair. From their cosmic cloth, he has made you a robe. . . ."

There's a subtle stir, and I look up and see him. He stands at the edge of the circle, eyes gently lowered, a tranquil presence. A cascade of turquoise and golden silk flows over his left arm. The Sisters are quiet, and the numinous atmosphere of the circle intensifies. A long moment passes as we all connect with him, breathe him in.

I Ching brings her hands to her heart and invites him into the circle with an almost imperceptible nod. He takes his time, lifts his ocean eyes to mine, seeking my consent. *Yes,* I nod. *Yes.*

He steps into the circle with a dancer's grace, long hair streaming over his shoulders. As he does so, I stand, feeling his grace pour into me. I've known him forever, yet I'm completely mystified by our reunion. I wonder how I've lived without him for so long. . . .

"He has always been with you," Chinese Medicine murmurs, and I realize the Sisters are standing. "Now, you can feel him again."

He moves to the center of the circle and faces me. Holding the robe in both hands, he lets it unfurl. Iridescence tumbles to the floor, turquoise waves of silk with a splash of golden light around the edges. He calls me to him with his eyes, the ecstasy of his return coursing through me. The space melts between us. He swings the robe, and with one smooth motion drapes me in the beauty of Heaven and Earth, a perfect fit.

River Eden Seeds
of Transformation

- Opportunities to dance with life are everywhere.

- Nature is a feast of beauty, pouring her magic into every moment of my life.

- Pleasure flows through me and transforms my experience of every moment.

- I fully receive the joy inherent in every moment.

- I embrace the fullness of my true nature.

- I receive loving help from the unseen world.

- My heart and mind, anima and animus, beloved and lover, are integrated within me.

- My inner beloved is a constant presence within me, always reflected in the people and things that open me to the joys of life.

- My inner beloved rides in on the pathways I've opened in my heart.

- My inner beloved is one with me, transforming the archetypal union between Heaven and Earth into an intimate love affair.

- I am draped in the beauty of Heaven and Earth, and it is a perfect fit.

PART II

22 *Essential Pearls*
from the
Three Sisters
of the *Tao*

Introduction
of the
22 Essential Pearls

The Essential Pearls are 22 meditative practices and activities that have been cultivated to enhance your experience of the Three Sisters. As introspective exercises, they can be practiced alone or shared with others. Each Pearl begins with a quotation from one of the Sisters, followed by the purpose for and guidance into the experience.

As the Sisters advise in all things, please take your time, hold each Pearl in your heart, and let it open you to the pleasures of exploring your inner world.

Please note: It can be beneficial to keep a journal as you step into this part of the journey. Choose one that really pleases you in every way, including size, color, and design. You may be drawn to a journal with lined or unlined paper, a particular size, one that provides a place for a pen, and so forth. Take your time, and let the process of making your choice be an enchanting one.

If you already keep a journal, consider beginning a new one dedicated to your experiences with the Three Sisters' Essential Pearls. You can also keep your notes on a computer. The truth is, you can have it be however you wish. . . .

CHAPTER FIVE

Essential Pearls
from
Chinese Medicine

Chinese Medicine views your true self as a convergence of Heaven and Earth. Harmony is gently held in place by a balanced lifestyle that encourages tranquility, sensuality, and creativity. In this atmosphere, your body and soul fully merge, love flourishes, and your true self thrives.

Essential Pearl #1:
Opening Your Gateways of Heaven and Earth

"The radiant essences of Heaven and Earth are always streaming around you, and now you are learning how to open your inner gateways and invite them to flow into you. As you

breathe, feel them flow into your body from above and below, merge in your heart, and expand out through every cell of your body and beyond. . . ."

Purpose: to open the heavenly and earthly gateways in your body.

Sit comfortably in a place where you have 15 minutes or more of quiet time.

Close your eyes and let your body relax more deeply with each breath. As you breathe, become aware of Earth's energy beneath you. Explore the qualities of this vibration. It may include a certain color or movement as it flows below you. Then, become aware of Heaven's energy, noticing its qualities as it moves above you.

When you're ready, inhale and visualize your pelvic area very gently opening to receive the earthly energies, rising up through your body and streaming into your heart. You may feel certain sensations, see particular colors or images, or have other experiences associated with Earth's essence, pleasantly flowing up and into your heart.

Inhale again and envision the top of your head gently opening to receive heavenly energies, streaming down through your body and blending with Earth's vibrations. Notice your sensory experiences—what you see, feel, hear, smell, or taste—as you observe the energies of Heaven and Earth merging and intermingling in your heart with every breath.

Bask here for as long as you wish.

Record your experience in your journal.

Essential Pearl #2: Your True Self, Revealed

"Your heart, the sanctuary of Heaven and Earth, is the home of your true self. . . . Through you, they are prolific! They cause inspiration and sensuality to merge within you, calling forth your true self. You begin to see the rolling landscapes of music, hear the poetry of paintings, savor the taste of colors, and revel in the fragrant bouquets of words. You become the explorer of your own endless wilderness. Their synergy within you enhances the potency of your work, the sensations in your body, and the depth of your inner sojourns."

Purpose: to fully ground and integrate your true self.

Sit comfortably in a place where you have 20 minutes or more of quiet time.

Begin with the meditation from Essential Pearl #1. Experience the heavenly and earthly energies flowing into you and merging in your heart. Their blending begins to shape and reveal your true self. Open yourself to experiencing the fullness of your true being as angel and animal entwined . . . a temple of miracles . . . a living altar of soul and cells . . . a creative genius illuminating cellular structure . . . a love child of Heaven and Earth. . . . Let these words come alive within you and bring feelings and images to the surface as you flow into the essence of who you truly are.

Bask here for as long as you wish.

Record your impressions and insights in your journal.

Suggestions for Deepening
Your True-Self Experience

— Gather images from magazines, picture books, and greeting cards that capture aspects of your true self. (Copy images you don't wish to remove from their sources.) You may wish to include nature objects, fabrics, and other meaningful components. Arrange them as a collage or work of art, and place your creation where you can see it daily. Gaze at it and allow it to speak to you as it enriches and deepens your experience of your true self. Let it be a dynamic creation that you can add to or change at any time, or create new art to express other aspects of your true self.

— Consider ways in which you can dress or adorn yourself to reflect your true essence. There may be certain colors, clothing, jewelry, or ways of styling your hair that are direct expressions of your authentic nature. Notice how you feel when you do this.

Essential Pearl #3: Your Circle of Belonging

"It begins with the remembrance of how love really feels. Incrementally, each memory and moment helps you reclaim your true nature; and as you do, your heart is restored. . . . Reunited once again with the full circle of life, your heart becomes the enchanted abode where Heaven and Earth's beloved offspring— you—can thrive."

Purpose: to establish an inner circle where you *feel* unconditionally loved.

Choose a place where you can relax comfortably and quietly for 30 minutes or more.

Begin by making note of those with whom you share a strong bond of love. Include anyone you know or have known, living or deceased, as well as beloved animals and unseen helpers. You can also include anyone you'd like to know but haven't met yet. You may identify a specific group of loved ones—such as classmates, club members, or families—who are best represented by one member within your Circle. Take your time, beginning with childhood and moving through the years to the present moment. Let love and gratitude guide your choices, and include only those with whom you share a deeply nurturing heart connection.

Once you've completed your list, close your eyes and visualize gathering with them in a close circle—your Circle of Belonging. Take the time to deeply connect with every member. The more you can tune in to and feel the potency of love you share with each one of them, the better.

You can bring your Circle together at any time. Consider gathering together daily as part of your meditation, or whenever you wish to feel their loving support.

Suggestions for Deepening Your
Circle-of-Belonging Experience

— Write each name on a piece of paper and arrange the pieces in a circle on a larger paper or board. Be as creative as you'd like with this, adding other elements such as colors, photos, images, and words to make your own Circle-of-Belonging collage. You may wish to keep this private or display it where you can see it often.

— Visualize members in your Circle interrelating. You may see them hugging, dancing, or talking with each other. Feel the love that flows among everyone as they connect with each other.

— Create a physical experience of your Circle by gathering any of the members together for meditation and/or conversation.

Check your Circle from time to time to determine if you'd like to make any changes, adding or removing members to sustain its potency.

Record your experiences in your journal.

Essential Pearl #4: Your Tapestry of Pleasure

"Harmony is made from the threads of pleasure you weave into your everyday experiences. The more these strands intricately embellish the matrix of your daily life, the better."

Purpose: to enrich and increase the pleasure quotient of your everyday life.

Set aside 30 minutes or more to contemplate and make note of what brings you pleasure. Take your time, feel into each query, and let your answers bubble up to the surface. . . .

— **Sight:** Recall who and what you take great pleasure in seeing. Include your favorite people; natural environments such as ocean or forest; human-made spaces and objects; colors, patterns, and shapes; and anything that visually nurtures and uplifts you.

— **Touch:** Consider who and what you most love to feel touching your skin, including your favorite people; fabrics; oils; and natural elements, such as sunlight and water. Describe the ways you most enjoy being touched by other people.

— **Taste:** Make note of your favorite tastes. Consider each of the seasons and the associated foods that you particularly enjoy during spring, summer, autumn, and winter, as well as the flavors you enjoy all year.

— **Smell:** List the scents that most please you. Give thought to your favorite food aromas, fragrances found in nature, the scents of your beloved ones, and the smells that inspire you and evoke fond memories.

— **Sound:** Make note of your favorite sounds, including those found in natural or human-made environments. Contemplate the music and voices you find most appealing.

After working with your five senses, develop a list of the activities and quiet pastimes that bring you the most pleasure.

Describe your ideal lifestyle, including the time you prefer to rise in the morning and retire in the evening, when you enjoy having your meals, and the general way in which you like your days and nights to unfold.

Study all of your notes and determine ways you can immediately bring more sensory pleasure into your everyday life. Notice the choices that may appear small—such as a particular type of flower on your desk, certain sheets on your bed, or specific aromatic herbs in your garden—have a way of enriching the pleasure quotient of your day. You may also decide to alter your schedule in order to make more time for the people, activities, or pastimes you cherish; or make other changes that bring you more joy. Lean into your preferences and observe how the pleasure they bring you enhances the overall quality of your life, including your creativity, vitality, and sensuality.

Remain open to all that brings you pleasure. As you focus on the many facets of your own joy, it manifests all around you.

Record your experiences and discoveries in your journal.

Essential Pearl #5:
The Trinity of Work, Rest, and Play

"Your work, rest, and play are a trinity of influences that all contribute to the tapestry of your life. By honoring them as equals, you balance the synergy of your body and spirit and restore the natural grace of <u>being</u> a human being."

Purpose: to restore or sustain a harmonious lifestyle.

Keep a log for three or more 24-hour cycles, recording the time you spend:

— **Working:** This means accomplishing time-dependent or other action-oriented tasks. Examples are employment, errands, chores, volunteering, and situations or conditions that require your actively focused energy.

— **Resting:** This includes being in peaceful repose, physically inactive, or in restorative sleep, as well as introspection and meditation.

— **Playing:** This is engaging in enjoyable activities and quiet pastimes that you find particularly inspiring or relaxing. These are typically not time dependent or stress related, and they offer you an opportunity to go with the flow. Examples include hobbies and creative projects, reading, pleasurable exercise, watching uplifting movies and television, and gathering with friends and family members whom you truly enjoy spending time with.

Although your log will be unique in content, look for a generally equal balance of work, rest, and play. If you find imbalances, consider how you can correct them. Let the changes you make, large or small, build more pleasure and fulfillment into your daily life.

Record your insights and experiences in your journal.

Refer to Essential Pearls #19 and #20 for an environmental approach to your work, rest, and play.

Essential Pearl #6:
Your Inner Sanctuary and Beyond

"Reclaim the wings of your imagination and ride the currents of feeling into your inner world. The sanctuary of your heart is not so much <u>thought</u> as <u>felt</u> into being. Fill it with love, love, and more love. . . . As you breathe life into your inner world, it takes on a vitality of its own. It breathes life back into you. . . . Be ever enchanted as you drink in the layers of astonishing beauty that your choices create. They are solely and eternally yours."

Purpose: to create an inner sanctuary of your own unique design where you're completely embraced by what makes your heart sing.

Choose a place where you can sit or lie down comfortably and in complete silence for 30 minutes or more.

Let your eyes gently close and take a few deep breaths, relaxing more with each one. As you let go, begin to imagine walking down a lovely path toward a spectacular pair of gates. Take your time in noting their beautiful details.

When you're ready, open the gates and step through into a paradise of your own making. This is a world where you can have everything be exactly the way you wish. No compromising, budgetary concerns, or dictates of any kind exist here. Let your inner sanctuary appear as a pure manifestation of the architecture, atmosphere, colors, fragrances, sounds, and textures you love. Explore the details in and around your internal haven, giving your imagination full reign to create (and re-create) a space that most pleases you.

Your inner sanctuary is the beginning point in the limitless world that exists within you, a realm you can explore and develop as much as you wish. It stretches out as far as you can imagine. This develops your creativity and enriches the inherent connection between your inner and outer worlds.

Suggestions for Deepening Your Inner-Sanctuary Experience

— Your inner sanctuary can become a gathering place for your Circle of Belonging (Essential Pearl #3), or you may choose to create another place that's specifically dedicated to that group.

— Collect images from magazines, picture books, and greeting cards that capture aspects of your interior paradise. (Make copies of images you don't wish to remove from their sources.) Consider including natural objects and other meaningful components and symbols. Arrange them as a collage or piece of art, and place your creation where you can see it daily. Feel into it and let it speak to you, enriching the experience of your inner world. Change or add to it as you feel the urge to do so.

— As your internal realm expands, consider creating places that meet specific needs or desires. You may wish to have an inner space such as a healing temple; an old-growth forest; a meditation garden; or specific areas dedicated to enhancing your wisdom, creativity, or sensuality.

Record your experiences and insights in your journal.

Essential Pearl #7: Seeds of Transformation

"As your tranquility deepens, the inspired brilliance of Heaven and the sweet sensuality of Earth integrate within you. You become luminosity and ecstasy entwined. Your capacity to embody love encircles you and stretches into all moments. This is your

future becoming present, your true self returning to the sanctuary of your heart. It is the Way."

Purpose: to nurture and sustain your true self.

Take ten minutes of quiet time and turn to Chinese Medicine's Seeds of Transformation at the end of Chapter 1. Choose one you'd like to live with for the day, and begin by contemplating the personal meaning of your chosen Seed. Use it as a portal into introspection, letting it spark your imagination, thoughts, feelings, and memories. Record your impressions, along with the Seed, in your journal.

Suggestions for Deepening Your
Seeds-of-Transformation Experience

— Write down the Seeds you resonate with and place them where you can see them throughout the day. Notice and record your impressions and responses.

— The Seeds can be points of inspiration for your creativity. Let them guide you in writing; playing music; creating a dance; or making a drawing, collage, painting, or other work of art.

CHAPTER SIX

Essential Pearls
from
I Ching

I Ching illuminates the loving union of your heart and mind. Her keynote is kindness, directing you to color every thought, word, and action with it; and to watch as kindness circles around and sows all manner of blessings into your life. She also unveils the nonphysical world of loving help devoted to your ever-unfolding transformation.

Essential Pearl #8:
The Loving Union of Your Heart and Mind

"The Way is inclusive, not exclusive. Your heart and mind are meant to be lovers, not enemies. Like Heaven and Earth,

they wish only to live as equals in harmony within you. It's their kind wisdom together, the sublime flow of their discerning devotion, that creates the loving world where you—the true you—can thrive."

Purpose: to regain or sustain the loving relationship between your heart and mind.

Sit or lie down comfortably in a place where you have 15 minutes or more of quiet time.

Close your eyes and let your body relax more deeply with each breath. Take your time. As you breathe, become aware of two orbs of light, one originating in your heart and the other in your mind. Watch them pulsate and brighten as you focus upon them. Imagine them expanding and blending together to form one larger orb of light, illuminating your entire body. Make note of your sensory experiences— what you see, feel, hear, smell, or taste—as you observe the beacons of your heart and mind merging, growing, and emanating from you. Visualize them remaining harmoniously unified throughout your daily life.

Bask here for as long as you wish.

Suggestions for Deepening Your Union-of-Heart-and-Mind Experience

— Expand this meditation to include your home, your community, your country, and the world. As the unified light of your heart and mind increases, imagine it harmoniously intermingling with other people, places, and things. Notice how you feel.

— Imagine your Circle of Belonging (Essential Pearl #3) or any person or place you wish to bless, being infused with the light that emanates from you.

— Visualize your heart and mind becoming dance partners. Study each one in great detail, and notice their unique qualities and characteristics as they hold each other and move together.

Record your experiences and insights in your journal.

Essential Pearl #9:
The Path of Kindness

"The Way is paved with loving-kindness—the essence of your heart and mind, your spirit and flesh, every inner and outer part of you, flowing together as equals in the dance of harmony. . . . Because you shape your world one thought, word, and deed at a time, you must choose every moment to be kind to yourself and others. Although it may seem laborious at first, it's imperative. Kindness reveals the Way. It's how you find the path home."

Purpose: to embody kindness in thought, word, and action.

Choose a quiet place where you can relax comfortably for 15 minutes or more.

Settle into the calm atmosphere surrounding you and begin with Essential Pearl #8, bringing your heart and mind into a loving union. Imagine a world steeped in kindness. What would it look and sound like? How would it feel? Imagine and feel your home being permeated with tender loving-kindness. Expand your experience to include the people in your neighborhood, community, and country. Feel and imagine compassion being given and received on streets and highways; and in homes, schools, and businesses everywhere. Let your experience expand to include the entire population of planet Earth emitting a unified aura of kindheartedness. Inhale your vision, and bask in the accompanying feelings.

Suggestions for Deepening Your Path-of-Kindness Experience

— Choose an hour to be your Hour of Kindness and practice thinking kind thoughts, saying kind words, and acting kindly. Notice when you drift away from your goal in any respect—in thoughts, words, or deeds—and readjust your course. Pay attention and make note of what happens within and around you as a result.

— Extend your Hour of Kindness for longer periods of time. Notice where or with whom it's easy to maintain your practice versus when it's difficult. Determine how you can upgrade your responses. Often, improving the sensory experience surrounding your challenge will help you. Review Essential Pearl #4 for inspiration. Or when challenged by someone, consider bringing him or her into the middle of your Circle of Belonging (Essential Pearl #3) to receive blessings from the group.

— Practice self-kindness. Make note of ten or more ways you can be kinder to yourself and put them into action.

Be sure to record your experiences and perceptions in your journal.

Essential Pearl #10: The Kiss of Language

"One of your most powerful tools is language. With it, you can kiss or kill your progress. Words are meant to express love, not destroy it. . . . As you choose words to 'kiss' the world around you, you call a new reality into being. You find that the benevolence of your chosen vocabulary is mirrored in your outer world, and you become enchanted by the continuum of kindness flowing through your everyday life. As you weave love and compassion into the auditory fabric of your days, you experience them circling around and returning the kiss. You feel them brushing against your skin. Your thoughts and words can be the portals through which Heaven on Earth manifests."

Purpose: to become fluent in the language of kindness.

Consider entering a period of "immersion training" where, as when learning a foreign language, you surround yourself with the language of kindness. During this period, attentively shape your inner dialogue as well as your speech to maintain a loving stream of consciousness. Make note of your various responses to your kind thoughts and words, such as a calm body, a positive frame of mind, and general lightness of being; as well as your response to unloving expressions. Also notice others' responses to your kind versus unkind thoughts and words.

As you become more proficient, experiment with shifting unpleasant situations to pleasant ones with your use of language. Speak always from the "glass half full" perspective. Practice formulating thoughts and words into blessings. Continue your immersion training until you automatically think and speak kindly, a true sign of fluency.

Keep a log of your discoveries and experiences in your journal.

Essential Pearl #11:
Life's Improvisational Theater

"Life is so much more enjoyable when you focus on the blessings rather than the challenges. Every moment can be like improvisational theater, where you take great pleasure in either observing or participating in each unique scene. People; places; things; and

the spontaneous arrangement of words, patterns, colors, sounds, tastes, scents, and feelings portray Creation in constant motion. No two seconds are exactly alike. You can sit back and watch the show or jump in, whatever suits you in the moment."

Purpose: to become an observant appreciator of life.

Viewing each moment of life as improvisational theater can build objectivity, turn harsh judgments into fluid observations, and enhance your fluency in the language of kindness. It also affords you the opportunity to appreciate the spontaneous and ever-changing nature of life.

· You can enter the theater at any time, as the production is always unfolding within and around you. Sit back and enjoy the show when you're shopping, driving, having dinner with friends, or attending any gathering. Simply relax and observe the cast of characters as they enter and exit the stage of life, shifting your perception to appreciate the endless diversity of this world.

Make note of your observations and experiences in your journal.

Essential Pearl #12:
Your Unseen Helpers

"You're meant to reach <u>in</u> for help, not <u>up,</u> and travel through life with an inner entourage of loving helpers who are best described as friends. . . . You can learn a lot about them by contem-

plating the qualities you love in your most cherished friends and family members. What attracts you to them?"

Purpose: to establish or deepen your relationship with your unseen helpers.

Sit comfortably in a place where you have 20 minutes or more of quiet time.

Take a few moments to breathe and relax. Let your attention softly focus on the people you love. Make a list of those who come to mind. (They may very well be in your Circle of Belonging, Essential Pearl #3.) Make note of the qualities you most treasure about each person. Study your notes and contemplate the attributes of your outer beloved ones as descriptions of your inner, nonphysical helpers.

The unseen world is quite fluid, and your inner partners manifest according to the needs of the moment. As they make themselves known to you, spend some time exploring your relationship with them. Tune in to their essence and qualities, and feel the loving connection you share with each one. Ask if they have a message for you. If they aren't already in your Circle of Belonging, you may wish to invite them to join you there.

Bask in this experience for as long as you wish.

Record your experiences and insights in your journal.

Essential Pearl #13:
Asking for Help

"The most challenging time to ask for help is the first time. The next most difficult is the second time, and so on. Your trust in your inner helpers can only be built through familiarity, and silence is where they reside. When you take the time to commune with them, you discover you're never alone. You surrender to the loving guidance they've always offered you. . . . Listen to them, let them inspire and delight you, and most of all . . . <u>feel</u> how much they love you."

Purpose: to ask for help whenever you wish for it.

Set aside 20 minutes or more where you can lie down or sit comfortably.

Breathe deeply, and feel your body becoming more relaxed with every breath. When you're ready, imagine stepping into the middle of your Circle of Belonging (Essential Pearl #3). You may wish to lie down or sit comfortably in the center of your Circle; or make eye contact, exchange hugs, or connect heart to heart with each member.

Let your entire being open to the abundant presence of unconditional love and support surrounding you. Immerse yourself in the healing energies of your Circle; feel the members' love permeating and strengthening you on all levels. Ask for the help you seek, knowing there's no concern too great or too small. You may notice one or more new individuals who are there to help you with a specific request.

Consider asking if anyone would like to give you a message. Open yourself to receive the loving guidance and help offered by any or all members, and express your gratitude for their assistance.

You can also place a loved one or any personal or collective circumstance or condition in the middle of your Circle to be surrounded by blessings of love, healing, and support.

Essential Pearl #14:
Seeds of Transformation

"When love is dancing through you, you embody the choreography of your true self and gracefully move to the rhythm of your inner knowing and outer circumstances. Because they're always changing, you fluidly improvise. You recognize when to lead or follow, give or receive, speak or listen, depending upon the moment. You glide and swirl, pause and turn, flowing in sync with the Way."

Purpose: to nurture and sustain your true self.

Take ten minutes of quiet time and turn to the Seeds of Transformation from I Ching at the end of Chapter 2. Choose one you'd like to contemplate throughout the day, and begin by reflecting on the personal meaning of your chosen Seed. Use it as a portal into introspection, letting it spark your imagination, thoughts, feelings, and memories. Record your impressions and insights, along with the Seed, in your journal.

Suggestions for Deepening Your Seeds-of-Transformation Experience

— Write out the Seeds you're especially drawn to and place them where you can see them throughout the day. Make note of your responses.

— The Seeds can be a point of inspiration for your creative imagination. As you read them, pay attention to which ones inspire you, and follow your inner prompting to write a poem; dance; play music; or make a collage, painting, or other work of art.

CHAPTER SEVEN

Essential Pearls
from
Feng Shui

Feng Shui encourages you to personally craft an environmental sanctuary that celebrates and honors your true self. By doing so, your inner and outer worlds become harmonious reflections of each other, resonant chords in a living symphony of sacred space inside the greater matrix of your community.

Essential Pearl #15: The Continuum of Love

"Transforming your everyday world begins with a shift in perception about yourself and your surroundings. . . . It begins with imagining the whole environment, natural and human-made, as

a continuum of love, encompassing the entire planet and beyond; all of it as inspiring, healing, and blessed as the structures and landscapes you call sacred sites. . . . When you feel the continuum of love, you discover the Way isn't just randomly dotted with the sacred; it's infused with it."

Purpose: to regain or sustain an optimal relationship with your environment.

Sit comfortably in a place where you have 20 minutes or more of quiet time.

Imagine being in your Circle of Belonging (Essential Pearl #3). Visualize everyone holding hands, with left palms turned up and right palms down. Feel loving energy pour into your left palm from the person on your left, circulating through your body, and flowing out through your right palm to the person on your right. Experience the current flowing and bathing the entire Circle in a continuum of love. Visualize the group energy radiating out in all directions, inter -connecting with other Circles around the world and infusing everyone and everything in a continuum of love. Feel your body, heart, mind, and spirit responding to the loving-kindness circulating through and around you.

Suggestions for Deepening Your
Continuum-of-Love Experience

— Share this meditation with a close friend, family member, or group.

— Sit quietly and connect with beloved friends or family members long-distance by imagining you're holding hands with them and feeling the continuum of love flowing between you and rippling out to the world. You may choose to synchronize yourself with your loved ones so that you're meditating at the same time.

— Meet with one or more of your nonphysical helpers during this meditation.

— Let the continuum of love inspire your creative genius. Write, draw, play music, dance, or express your responses in a way that pleases you.

Record your insights and experiences in your journal.

Essential Pearl #16: Your Beloved Belongings

"Beloved belongings reflect and affirm who you are. They nurture your true self. There's a reason they're called <u>belongings</u>— you belong together. . . . Just imagine having such a loving

relationship with everything in your surroundings, a choir of harmonious voices all around you."

Purpose: to identify and appreciate the belongings that nurture and sustain you.

Find a comfortable place in your home to sit quietly for ten minutes or more. Look around and choose one object that you especially love. If you see nothing you have such an affinity with, bring a book, memento, or other beloved item to where you're sitting. Take a few minutes to make note of the qualities and associations that make this belonging so meaningful to you. Let it speak to you. How did it come into your life? Does it hold favorite memories? What are the feelings it awakens within you?

By contrast, focus on (or think of) a possession you don't like. Make note of the qualities and associations that are unattractive to you. Let it also speak to you. How did it come into your life? Does it hold any unpleasant memories? What are the feelings it elicits in you? Decide if, when, and how you can kindly let it go.

Record your experiences and insights in your journal.

Suggestions for Deepening Your
Beloved-Belongings Experience

— Repeat this exercise throughout your home, focusing on various possessions and the thoughts and feelings they

bring forth in you. As you identify items you don't resonate with, decide how you can kindly release them. When
obtaining new belongings, be conscious of choosing only
those "who" make your heart sing.

— Look through magazines, catalogs, and books and collect images of spaces and things you're particularly drawn to.
You may find that you're attracted to certain colors, styles,
and items over and over again. Place your collection in a
notebook or scrapbook and add to it as you find images you
love. Refer to it as you acquire new belongings.

Essential Pearl #17: Everything Counts

*"Shift the hierarchical mind-set that insists some things
merit better care than others, and level the playing field. Instead
of classifying your possessions by a certain pecking order, simply
give a good home to everything you love and need; and honor the
rest by letting it go. This, more than anything, strengthens the
continuum of love and harmony in your life."*

Purpose: to create a calm, clear living environment that
encourages and supports the full expression of your true self.

Set aside some uninterrupted time to walk through
your living or working space. Go slowly and approach this
from a meditative perspective. Make note of any cluttered or

disorganized areas and be aware of how you respond to them, noticing where you feel irritated, confused, or overwhelmed as you go. When you feel this way, spend a few moments visualizing the space in perfect condition, knowing your imagination is beginning the process of restoring order. Include cabinets; closets; drawers; and other storage areas such as the attic, basement, or garage in your survey.

If there's more than one area needing to be returned to order, consider where you feel most drawn to begin and schedule time to do so.

Label three boxes or bags:

1. Throw away
2. Give away
3. Put away

Ask the following questions about the items in the space and place them in the appropriate container until the area is clear.

- Do I love it?

- Do I need it?

- Does it support who I am now?

- Does it elicit pleasant or unpleasant memories or associations?

❷   Do I wish to continue to share my space with it?

❷   Do I own duplicates I can let go of?

❷   Does it need repair, and am I willing to restore it to its best condition now?

❷   If I'm letting it go, will I sell, lend, or give it away; and when? (The sooner you do so, the better.)

Be introspective as you approach this sorting process, knowing you're clearing space for more joy, love, and creativity to stream into your surroundings. When you've separated all items into one of the three categories:

1.   Immediately place the throw-away contents in the trash.

2.   Move or send the give-away things to their new homes (friends, family members, charity, and so on) as quickly as possible.

3.   Organize and store the put-away items, giving everything a good home.

When organizing the things you're keeping, it's helpful to have the shelves and containers necessary to properly house them. Often, these aren't required to be decorative, just functional. Group like items together, such as garden tools, sports equipment, hobby supplies, and memorabilia. Put the same types of clothing together in closets, such as shirts, jackets, slacks, and accessories. Follow this strategy in bedroom drawers, kitchen cabinets, and linen closets. Label containers if necessary. Your goal is to organize your possessions so that you can easily find what you're looking for, thus eliminating the confusion, "overwhelm," or irritation that can erode the quality of your life.

Make note of your experiences and insights in your journal.

Essential Pearl #18:
Your Environment as a Living Body

"Hierarchical mind-sets attempt to arrange things vertically, from most to least important. . . . When some areas are neglected while others are lavished with attention, harmony is lost in the grinding imbalance. Each room and space in your home serves a unique function, much like the organs in your body. Treat every square inch with the same dignity, knowing that together they all form the living body of your home."

Purpose: to attune to your surroundings as a living body.

This is best done either in concert with Essential Pearl #17 or after you've completed it. Set aside some quiet time to walk through your home (or another place where you spend time). Notice whether you consider some areas more important than others. If you find this is true, spend some time in those spots you consider "less than" and tune in to their essence. Make note of the functions they serve, or could serve. Imagine how they'd look and feel when optimally meeting those purposes. Decide how you can begin to bridge the gap between the current and the ideal conditions of these spaces. This may include a new coat of paint, different furniture or decor, a change in lighting, or other alterations.

Suggestions for Deepening Your Environment-as-a-Living-Body Experience

— Stand or sit in an area you previously considered unimportant and listen to what it has to say. Tune in to the voice of the space and invite it to guide you in bringing it to its optimal condition.

— Become aware of any changes within yourself as you approach your entire environment with loving-kindness. Make note of your feelings and discoveries in your journal.

— If you haven't named your abode, consider doing so. Tune in to it as a living body "who" shelters and protects you. It has a name if you choose to know it. . . .

Essential Pearl #19:
Habitats for Work, Rest, and Play

"You and your home share a living partnership. Each abode presents its own possibilities for meeting your needs. Together, you co-create the physical spaces that hold your work, rest, and play in place, assuring your harmony. . . .

"Work can be loud and demanding. It's best given its own dedicated space where you can close a door, sprawl out, and be productive without compromising other areas of the house. . . . Rest can be anchored in any quiet spot, such as a comfortable chair in a private room or alcove—a place where you can retreat from the insistent voices of the computer, exercise equipment, or television. Rest's native habitat is in your bedroom, where the bed reigns and sensual play is invited in like a lover. . . .

"Let your playfulness waft gently through the quiet areas and parade boldly through active spaces in the house. Play carries the imaginative surge that can inspire your productivity and deepen your rest."

Purpose: to identify your individual environmental needs and establish or refine places to meet those needs.

Set aside 30 minutes of uninterrupted time. Begin by assessing how well your environment meets your *current* work, rest, and play needs. You may wish to make notes about your findings.

Concerning your work space(s), ask:

❷ Is it sufficiently organized?

❷ Is my desk, table, or working surface the correct size for me?

❷ Do I have enough storage space?

❷ How comfortable is my work chair?

❷ Is this an attractive, inspiring place to be?

❷ Do I have the privacy I need?

❷ Can I shut a door or in some way remove myself from the area when I choose to?

Concerning your rest space(s), ask:

❷ Is my bedroom dedicated to my rest and relaxation?

❷ Is it an attractive, tranquil place to be?

❷ Is it sufficiently organized and private?

❷ Does it contain anything that may compromise my rest, such as a computer, exercise equipment, or TV?

◑ If so, would my bedroom be more peaceful if I relocated that item to another spot?

◑ Are there other quiet areas in the house where I can relax, read, or meditate?

◑ If not, is there an area I can devote to quietude?

Concerning your play space(s), ask:

◑ Do I have one or more places in the house that are dedicated to my favorite ways to play?

◑ How does my fun-loving spirit manifest in my work space?

◑ How is my playfulness revealed in my bedroom?

◑ How are these energies expressed in my dining area?

◑ Do other areas in my home express a lightness of being?

◑ If so, specifically how?

◑ If not, how might I bring more playfulness into these spots?

The answers to these questions will guide you in making the changes that can balance and enhance your areas related to work, rest, and play. Take your time and approach this as a dynamic process that's always unfolding—an environmental journey best enjoyed one step at a time.

Essential Pearl #20: Your Font of Creativity

"Once you've brought your surroundings into resonant order, the energy really gets going, and guess what happens? Your true self goes wild! With your inner and outer worlds aligned, you become a flowing font of creativity; and your environment becomes one of your favorite playgrounds. . . . A home is meant to sing the songs of the people who live there, the original music inspired by their unique interpretations of life. Your creativity is the signature of Heaven and Earth. When it comes calling, let it in!"

Purpose: to encourage your creativity to flow and be fully expressed in your environment.

Choose a quiet place where you can relax comfortably for 15 minutes or more. Contemplate how you'd describe your personal font of creativity. How do you love to express yourself? Let memories, images, colors, words, and qualities arise as you consider this. Make note of your findings in your journal.

When you're ready, take a walk through your surroundings and notice where your creativity is evident. Knowing that it's a direct manifestation of your true self, ask:

☯ Are there more ways I can express myself in my surroundings?

☯ Is there a space or room I can dedicate to my creative journey?

As you move through the space, make note of your observations. Discover where you feel drawn to make creative changes, such as rearranging furniture; adding or eliminating certain colors, art, or decor items; or changing the way the space is used.

Suggestions for Deepening Your Font-of-Creativity Experience

— You may find there are ways you'd like to be creative that require more room than you have at home. If so, do your best to make your dream come true by finding the space and fully stepping into your desired forms of expression. Whether it's a large art studio, dance floor, or kitchen, be innovative in finding your place . . . to be creative!

— Nurture the imagination of others. Encourage the people in your life to tap into their font of creativity and express themselves. Consider organizing group sessions to enjoy being with friends and family while engaging in activities that support this.

— Take time on a regular basis to determine if you have a longing for new expression. Be sensitive to and act on such a desire, knowing it's coming from the depths of your true self.

Essential Pearl #21: Seeds of Transformation

"Honor all of who you are. Live with what you love, and let everything else continue its journey. Celebrate your passions and pleasures and give them places to thrive in the paradise of your own making. Cherish the sacred essence in everyone and everything. You're here to experience a continuum of love as vast as you can imagine. It is the Way."

Purpose: to nurture and sustain your true self.

Take ten minutes of quiet time and turn to the Seeds of Transformation from Feng Shui at the end of Chapter 3. Choose a Seed to contemplate for the day, and begin by reflecting on its personal meaning. Use it as a portal into introspection, letting it inspire your imagination, thoughts, and feelings. Record the Seed along with your impressions in your journal.

Suggestions for Deepening Your
Seeds-of-Transformation Experience

— Choose Seeds you resonate with and place them where you can read them throughout the day.

— The Seeds can be points of inspiration for your creativity. As you read them, pay attention to your responses and follow your inner prompting to write; play music; or make a collage, painting, or other work of art.

CHAPTER EIGHT

An
Essential Pearl
from
River Eden

River Eden symbolizes your inner beloved. As you claim the fullness of your true self, you inevitably balance and integrate your inner and outer worlds, heart and mind, anima and animus, lover and beloved. You become whole within yourself.

Essential Pearl #22:
Your Inner Beloved

"All along, you've chosen friends and lovers who offer you a glimpse of he-who-is-you. He reveals himself in all that pleases you. As you've learned to recognize and appreciate him, he shows

117

himself more and more. He's a constant presence within you, always reflected in the people and things that turn your head, attract you, and open you to the joys of life. . . . All of who he is, you are. He's the inner side of your true self, riding in on the pathways you've opened within. He's joining you again, transforming the archetypal union between Heaven and Earth into an intimate affair."

Purpose: to explore and expand your relationship with your inner beloved.

Sit comfortably in a place where you have 30 minutes or more of quiet time. Have a pen and two pieces of paper or your journal handy.

Settle into a tranquil atmosphere, relaxing more deeply with every breath. As you do so, consider the people you know or have known who possess qualities and characteristics that are compellingly attractive to you. Beginning as far back as you can remember, write down the relatives, teachers, friends, neighbors, boy- or girlfriends, lovers, bosses, colleagues, movie stars, and acquaintances who have made a powerful, positive impact on you. They can be any age or gender, and may or may not be in your Circle of Belonging (Essential Pearl #3).

Make a list of their attributes on another piece of paper. These may be physical characteristics you find particularly beautiful or handsome, temperaments and abilities you're quite drawn to, or other attractive traits. (If you have a mixed response to someone you'd like to include, please note only the positive aspects.)

Take a few moments to study your list of attributes. They open a personal portal into the essence of your inner beloved, the he- (or she-) who-is-you. The qualities you find most compellingly attractive in others reflect the inner facets of your true self.

Suggestions for Deepening Your Inner-Beloved Experience

— If your list includes physical characteristics, imagine them describing your inner beloved. Close your eyes and visualize him or her approaching you. You may wish to make eye contact or talk with this being, or embrace and feel the blending of your energies.

— Develop an ever-deepening relationship by including your inner beloved in your Circle of Belonging, meditations, or inner dialogues. Take the time to continue to explore and integrate the qualities he or she offers you.

— Circle the attributes on your list that currently describe *you*. Then look at those you haven't marked, choose the one that's most compelling, and practice embodying it in the world. Return to your list from time to time and select another attribute for the same purpose.

— Collect images that capture aspects of your inner beloved, often found in magazines, books, and greeting cards. (Copy images you don't wish to remove from their sources.) Your creation can be as symbolic or literal as you choose; and can include components such as nature objects, fabrics, and other meaningful items or symbols. Arrange the items as a collage or other work of art. Let your creation speak to you and deepen your relationship with your inner beloved. Follow the slipstream of your creativity as you're inspired by your experiences.

Afterword

Our future rests in the arms of our true selves. Every one of our compassionate thoughts, words, and deeds contributes to our individual and collective evolution. With both seen and unseen help, we can transform all violent, disconnected, heartless responses into the steadfast experience of love and respect for all of Creation.

Embodying tranquility, sensuality, and kindness, we step off the hierarchical ladder and into our Circle of Belonging. As transmitters of love, our heartfelt intentions flow through us like crystalline water cascading over precious stones. As Heaven and Earth entwined, we channel love into form—love for our bodies, our planet, and our lives. Together, we imagine it, feel it, and make it so.

It is the Way.

Acknowledgments

As an author, I disappear into the depths of writing and sometimes don't resurface for quite a while. When I do come up for air, I'm often a bit disoriented and need to check my direction. To do this, I look to those who help me stay on course. They're all beacons of light in my life, love children of Heaven and Earth who illuminate my world.

Brian Collins, whom I call "Briangel" because he is, has inspired me for years with his unwavering kindness toward all beings. Always impressed by and drawn to his benevolent ways, I now appreciate them as the Way. His tender loving-kindness permeates my life, much as his perceptive editing permeates this book.

A pod of soul sisters swam beside me as I headed into the oceanic world of the Three Sisters, their love and blessings buoying me along the way. My familial bond with these women wraps me in the grace of a loving sisterhood, a true circle of belonging.

Meo O'Malley carefully read the manuscript many times, feeling into the heart of the Sisters with me, sharing her intuitive brilliance and bringing possibilities to my attention that often transformed the content. Her luminous spirit can be found on every page.

Laurel Aarsvold, Barbra Dillenger, Jackee Earnest, Dianne Franks, Gita Gendloff, Shivam and Apara Kohls, Marylou LoPreste, Mimi Miller, Beatrex Quntana, Cheryl Rice, Barbara Richards, and Barbara Takashima each blessed me with their patient understanding of my frequent disappearances and writer's quirks, and helped me navigate through the mysteries of an evolving manuscript with their generous presence and insightful feedback.

Louise Hay knew exactly when to show up and drag me outside for a cup of tea. We sat in the garden and laughed about the latest antics in the improvisational theater of life, and I always returned to my desk feeling refreshed and inspired.

Jo'Ann Ruhl, whose no-nonsense astrological wisdom has guided me over the years, channeled the essence of the Three Sisters when she said, "You better start feeling your feelings or you are going to miss the rest of your life!" Like the Sisters, she has a way of saying exactly the right words at the right time.

My Essential Feng Shui team: Karen Carrasco, Amy Chini, Becky Iott, and Liv Kellgren, steadfastly take tender loving care of the Western School of Feng Shui, and share with me a keen interest in the union of creativity and education. We share a bounty of memories and simply couldn't make up the impromptu classroom "theater" we've experienced together.

My sister Carol Beatson, the mistress of optimism, remains one of my most enthusiastic cheerleaders. My depiction of Feng Shui in these pages captures a bit of her effervescent spirit.

The juicy friendships I share with my soul brothers give me plenty of opportunity to enjoy the beauty and magic of men. Each contributed to the experience I describe in Chapter 4. Poet and visionary futurist Gary Sycalik heartens me with his loving support and sagacious perceptions, uplifting and inspiring me along the Way. Cute neighbor Dan Cool, also my sound and computer champion, insists on immersing me in very sensual music, transforming my writing experience from silent to sensational. My fellow water dragon Randal McEndree shares my love of dance and taught me the indispensable skill of folding my feet. Matthew Aarsvold, Bill Crane, Richard Earnest, Michael Makay, and Dan McFarland, partners of some of my soul sisters, continually delight me with their charm, depth, and brilliance.

I deeply appreciate the patience and understanding of everyone at Hay House as I journeyed through a time that simply couldn't be rushed.

Authors Carol Anthony, Doc Childre, Gregory Colbert, Lorie Eve Dechar, Esther and Jerry Hicks, Trebbe Johnson, Howard Martin, Hanna Moog, Thomas Moore, Neville (aka Neville Goddard), Dr. Christiane Northrup, John O'Donohue, and David Whyte stirred me up, set me reeling, enchanted me with their words, and fueled my creativity with their works listed in Sources of Inspiration at the end of this book.

All of these kindred spirits mirror the help I receive from my nonphysical friends. I'm forever grateful to the Three Sisters and a host of unseen helpers who lovingly guide me along the Way.

Sources
of
Inspiration

I Ching: The Oracle of the Cosmic Way, and all other works by Carol Anthony and Hanna Moog

The HeartMath Solution, and all other works by Doc Childre and Howard Martin

Ashes and Snow, a novel in letters, and all other works by Gregory Colbert

Five Spirits: Alchemical Acupuncture for Psychological and Spiritual Healing, and all other works by Lorie Eve Dechar

Ask and It Is Given: Learning to Manifest Your Desires, and all other works by Esther and Jerry Hicks

The World Is a Waiting Lover: Desire and the Quest for the Beloved, and all other works by Trebbe Johnson

The Re-Enchantment of Everyday Life, and all other works by Thomas Moore

Resurrection, and all other works by Neville (aka Neville Goddard)

The Secret Pleasures of Menopause, and all other works by Christiane Northrup, M.D.

Eternal Echoes: Exploring Our Hunger to Belong, and all other works by John O'Donohue

The House of Belonging, and all other works by David Whyte

About the Author

Terah Kathryn Collins is a best-selling author and the founder of the Western School of Feng Shui (**www.wsfs.com**). She's the originator of Essential Feng Shui®, which focuses on the many beneficial applications of Feng Shui in our Western culture while honoring the essence of its Eastern heritage. Her books on the subject have sold more than a million copies worldwide.

Her current work centers on embodying the Tao. She may be contacted by visiting: **www.3sistersofthetao.com**.

An
Invitation

The conversation continues.
It courses through every heart
Seeking the sound of other hearts
Opening
I invite you to share your experiences
of this material with me:
www.3sistersofthetao.com

Sharing the Journey,

Terah Kathryn Collins

Hay House Titles of Related Interest

YOU CAN HEAL YOUR LIFE, the movie,
starring Louise L. Hay & Friends
(available as a 1-DVD program and an expanded 2-DVD set)
Watch the trailer at: **www.LouiseHayMovie.com**

THE SHIFT, the movie,
starring Dr. Wayne W. Dyer
(available as a 1-DVD program and an expanded 2-DVD set)
Watch the trailer at: **www.DyerMovie.com**

☯ ☯ ☯

The Age of Miracles: *Embracing the New Midlife,*
by Marianne Williamson

The Answer Is Simple . . . *Love Yourself, Live Your Spirit!*
by Sonia Choquette

The Art of Extreme Self-Care: *Transform Your Life
One Month at a Time,* by Cheryl Richardson

The Astonishing Power of Emotions: *Let Your Feelings Be Your Guide,*
by Esther and Jerry Hicks (The Teachings of Abraham®)

The Secret Pleasures of Menopause Playbook: *A Guide to Creating
Vibrant Health Through Pleasure,* by Christiane Northrup, M.D.

28 Days to a More Magnetic Life, by Sandra Anne Taylor

All of the above are available at your local bookstore,
or may be ordered by contacting Hay House (see next page).

☯ ☯ ☯

We hope you enjoyed this Hay House book. If you'd like to receive our online catalog featuring additional information on Hay House books and products, or if you'd like to find out more about the Hay Foundation, please contact:

Hay House, Inc., P.O. Box 5100, Carlsbad, CA 92018-5100

(760) 431-7695 or (800) 654-5126
(760) 431-6948 (fax) or (800) 650-5115 (fax)
www.hayhouse.com® • www.hayfoundation.org

Published and distributed in Australia by: Hay House Australia Pty. Ltd., 18/36 Ralph St., Alexandria NSW 2015 • *Phone:* 612-9669-4299 • *Fax:* 612-9669-4144 • www.hayhouse.com.au

Published and distributed in the United Kingdom by: Hay House UK, Ltd., 292B Kensal Rd., London W10 5BE • *Phone:* 44-20-8962-1230 • *Fax:* 44-20-8962-1239 • www.hayhouse.co.uk

Published and distributed in the Republic of South Africa by: Hay House SA (Pty), Ltd., P.O. Box 990, Witkoppen 2068 • *Phone/Fax:* 27-11-467-8904 • info@hayhouse.co.za • www.hayhouse.co.za

Published in India by: Hay House Publishers India, Muskaan Complex, Plot No. 3, B-2, Vasant Kunj, New Delhi 110 070 • *Phone:* 91-11-4176-1620 • *Fax:* 91-11-4176-1630 • www.hayhouse.co.in

Distributed in Canada by: Raincoast, 9050 Shaughnessy St., Vancouver, B.C. V6P 6E5 • *Phone:* (604) 323-7100 *Fax:* (604) 323-2600 • www.raincoast.com

Take Your Soul on a Vacation

Visit **www.HealYourLife.com®** to regroup, recharge, and reconnect with your own magnificence. Featuring blogs, mind-body-spirit news, and life-changing wisdom from Louise Hay and friends.

Visit **www.HealYourLife.com** today!

HEAL YOUR LIFE ♥

Take Your Soul on a Vacation

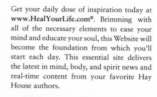

Get your daily dose of inspiration today at **www.HealYourLife.com®**. Brimming with all of the necessary elements to ease your mind and educate your soul, this Website will become the foundation from which you'll start each day. This essential site delivers the latest in mind, body, and spirit news and real-time content from your favorite Hay House authors.

Make It Your Home Page Today!
www.HealYourLife.com®

www.hayhouse.com®